"Think How They Think To Do What We Do"

—Douglas Davis

This is your brain on strategy in custom Spencerian script. It's a beautiful mind.
thinkhowtheythink.com

BOOKS

HOW BOOKS
An Imprint of Simon & Schuster, Inc.
57 Littlefield Street
Avon, Massachusetts 02322

For information about special discounts for bulk purchases, please contact Simon & Schuster Special Sales at 1-866-506-1949 or business@ simonandschuster.com.

The Simon & Schuster Speakers Bureau can bring authors to your live event. For more information or to book an event contact the Simon & Schuster Speakers Bureau at 1-866-248-3049 or visit our website at www.simonspeakers.com.

Manufactured in the United States of America

10 9 8 7 6 5

Library of Congress Cataloging-in-Publication Data has been applied for.

ISBN 978-1-4403-4155-7
ISBN 978-1-4403-4161-8 (ebook)

Cover letterform design © Tony Di Spigna.
Interior art by Douglas Davis.
Diagrams in Chapter 8 by Judy Abel.
Tactical and strategic images in Chapter 9 by Rick Redznak.
Interior cartoon by Tom Fishburne, Marketoonist, *www.marketoonist.com*.

CREATIVE STRATEGY

AND THE

BUSINESS OF DESIGN

DOUGLAS DAVIS

HOW Books
New York London Toronto Sydney New Delhi

ACKNOWLEDGMENTS

A lot of people thank God because they couldn't have done it without Him. As a child, I fell out of a moving car into an intersection. As a young adult, I battled addiction. As an adult, I abandoned my portfolio to escape a fireball when a second plane hit a building two blocks away from me. Without God, I know I wouldn't even be here. Thank you. To my grandparents, Ben Frank & Sarah Mae Davis, my first teachers. When you were here, I watched and learned from you every day. My students don't know that they are also your students. Thank you. To my mother, Audrey Faye Davis, my protector. I watched as you sacrificed everything for Marlon and me growing up. Without the letters you wrote to an unruly teenager, and the mail-order art school lessons you couldn't afford, I wouldn't be here. Thank you. To my design mentor and example of how to give to students, Typographer and Distinguished Professor Tony Di Spigna. As a master typographer, I aspire toward your level of passion, creativity, and dedication. Sixteen years after I graduated from Pratt, you still give your time, advice, and willingness long after your obligation to do so ended. Thank you. To my strategy mentor and example of how to engage the minds of my students, Dr. Marjorie Kalter. Your distinguished agency career, competitive strategy insights, and encouragement to "just get through it" helped me focus when I couldn't see the way forward. You had a profound influence on what I do, and as a result, I am relevant to clients in a whole new way. Thank you. To my contributors Neil Feinstein, Barry Silverman, Andrea Waite-Spurlock, Judy Abel, and Ron Berger, you were my first and only choices for your areas of expertise. I continue to learn from you and I'm so grateful that the readers will as well. Thank you.

In early 2012, I was contacted by Laura Yoo, Content Development Manager for the Design Community at F+W Media, and from there I wrote Creative Strategy and the Business of Design course for HOW Design University. As a result, Sarah Whitman and Karli Petrovic were open to my articles based on the CSBD content, then Kathy Scott and Erin Semple Morrarty provided guidance when I turned the content into a webinar, while Amanda Malek, Alison Prior, and Jinnie Compton supported me and the many students in the course on HOWU. If not for Marketing Mentor Ilise Benun inviting me to speak within the Creative Business track of HOW Design Live (in Boston 2014, then Chicago 2015), I wouldn't have seen the impact of the content in real life or met superstar event planners Amy Conover, Sally Slack, or Michael Sauer, to then pitch the idea of this book to Scott Francis and Bridgid Agricola (thank you for the privilege of speaking at HDL in Atlanta 2016) or had the chance to work with my big-picture editor Brendan O'Neill, or laugh in between the lines with Laura Daly (thank you for the care with the material and willingness to learn about me in order to know how to extend the CSBD brand into book form). Thanks Amanda Aszman for the opportunity to be one of the judges of HOW's Promotion and Marketing Design Awards 2016. Thanks, Jess Zafarris, for giving me an outlet on HOWdesign .com. All of that is to say to HOW's publisher Gary Lynch, none of this would have happened without God's gift to me through these people. Thank you. To the design community, the HOW community, you took time out to answer my call for relevant problems from relevant professionals. Emely Perez, Anthony Clarke, Nora Elbaz, Kendell Burton, Joshua Namdar, Travis Bonilla, Rick Redznak, Intan Trenggana, Dimitri Alexander, Kacy Charles, Fabiola Veronica, Hajime Yoshida, Mervet Hafez, Hang Z., Shayne Alexander, Danny Shaw, Antoine Christian, Peter Shleykher, David Quintiliani, Janice Arroyo, Carol Chu, Claire Giddings, Eric O'Toole, Botond Vörös, Coco Cerrella, Mariam Guessous, Michael J. Miraflor, Andy Long, Chemene Phillips, Steven Brodeur, Rashi Puri, M. Genevieve Hitchings, Louisa McCabe, Carrie Hamilton, Ellen Baryshev, Niyati Mehta, Nakita M. Pope, Sean DallasKidd, Nick Matarese, Roxie Munro, Damien Golden, Tom N. Tumbusch, Michelle Muhammad, Ed Roberts, Lidia Varesco Racoma, Bryan Troche, Nancy Ruzow, Shannel Wheeler, Blake Winfree, Julius Dunn, Nicte Cuevas, Jacob Cass, and Gail Anderson. Though I couldn't fit all of the assignments in print format, thank you for the assignments that will help so many who are not located in a city with a large design community.

To my former professors in the Masters in Integrated Marketing program, as I learned the curriculum from you, I experienced what it meant to be taught by NYU professors. I attended Dr. Kalter's capstone class with the mindset that it was my job interview and being asked to join the faculty among you on graduation day in 2010 was one of the most validating days of my career. Your example is what I aspired to during my time at NYU. To my cohort at NYU, iron sharpens iron. Thank you for making me better, Veena Ramesh, Gabriela Urvina, Lenny Vyater, Aditi Kapadia, Robert McCutcheon, Ping Pan, and Husbi Ahmed, and a special thanks to Sally Shapiro and Kyla Malone for being there to bounce things off of in a pinch. Thanks to Fred Nickols for allowing me to use your Strategy-Execution Matrix, and to Tom Fishburne, the Marketoonist, for the laughs I've had over the years from 8 Types of Creative Critics. To my dependable, talented, and loyal squad of freelancers, Rick Redznak, Danny Shaw, Travis Bonilla, Anthony Clarke, Hajime Yoshida, and Horace Maxwell: without you there would be no Davis Group. Thank you.

To the Department of Communication Design faculty at New York City College of Technology, thank you for the outlet and freedom to do what I do. I'm amazed to see how much we accomplish with so little. I'm inspired by your commitment to providing a public avenue to an industry with a high barrier to entry. Thank you MaryAnn Biehl for your leadership, your sacrifice, and the flexibility to write this book. Special thanks to Professors Joel Mason and Bob Holden for taking a chance on a twenty-five-year-old kid with two years out of Pratt and three years in the field. Fourteen years later I'm grateful to serve our students alongside you at the foot of the Brooklyn Bridge. To the Masters in Professional Studies in the Branding and Integrated Communications (BIC) program at the City College of New York, thank you for my outlet on the graduate level. To Nancy Tag, whose vision and dedication has built something really unique from the curriculum to the distinguished faculty, thank you for your trust. Thank you Dana Miller at Gotham Writers Workshop for finding my freelance editor Clifford Thompson, who helped me with shaping the manuscript before I submitted it to HOW. Big thanks to Ryan Britt's Essay & Opinion class at Gotham—wow, that class with those characters was worth double what I paid (please don't double your prices). To my 206 family of friends and Fine and Performing Arts Department at Hampton University and my Brooklyn brothers and sisters Nikhil, Janice, Pelin, Chad, Sanders and Tam from Pratt Institute. You were my support system then and you are my support system now. To Luke Sullivan and Pete Barry, thank you for writing the words that help me help my students. I hope that this book becomes to others what your books have been to me in the classroom.

To my students, the reason I am here, you are my wealth. I am your biggest fan and will be here for you until I'm cold and dead in the grave—e-mail *me@douglasdavis .com*. You make me proud when you do your best, not because you succeed or win. Take advantage of your learning environments no matter what form they come in because your education is your winning lottery ticket, your NBA draft, your NFL draft. Compete with yourself. Help others. Use what you've learned. Stick together. Make sure they know Brooklyn is in the building. Push. Lead. Rise. Grind. #getit Thank you to my wife Janelle for being here for the adventure that is our life. The last five years have been a whirlwind of work and play for us both and I'm proud to see you finally reach your Broadway dream. Last but not least, thank God for my statistics tutor Michael Malenbaum.

CONTENTS

PART I | A DESIGNER CAUGHT IN THE HEADLIGHTS: CREATIVE BUSINESS SOLUTIONS

PART IV STAYIN' ALIVE: BUILDING A SUCCESSFUL CAREER

" It's been said that a picture is worth a thousand words. In the hands of the right designer, a word is worth a thousand pictures. **"**

—TONY DI SPIGNA,
Typographer and Distinguished Professor

FOREWORD BY
DR. MARJORIE KALTER

In *Creative Strategy and the Business of Design*, Douglas Davis provides "creatives"—designers, art directors, copywriters, and content providers—with a framework for their concepts to succeed. This higher level of success entails understanding and achieving the business objectives of the design project. As he writes in the Introduction, "Let's start with what we weren't taught." With this book, designers have a guide that fills in gaps for skills that aren't the subject matter of design school or the focus of internships, freelance work, or company training programs. That's because these skills haven't been considered essential or even appropriate for a creative role.

Awards for advertising effectiveness used to be rare; daily, weekly, and monthly measurement of a campaign's achievement of its goals used to be the purview of direct marketers. But that was the past. The proliferation of data has made it a possibility as well as a responsibility for every professional in the field of marketing communications to understand how business goals are set and how they are measured. With the growth of digital marketing, social media, and the technology for data collection, management, and analysis,

data can and should be part of the brief for every campaign. Chief Marketing Officers, brand managers, product managers, and entrepreneurs have dashboards on their laptops and tablets to track quantitative campaign response and qualitative trend data. Market research to elicit survey data can be conducted online. Consumer and even business-to-business response through social media is immediate—sometimes it's so rapid and dramatic that new or incremental design work is needed right away.

It is no longer sufficient for a campaign to be a big idea that generates awareness. To be successful, it has to be on strategy, trend positively with its target audience, and meet the projected metrics. When the design-school approach isn't matched by keen attention to the business goals, the campaign is at risk. The business may also be at risk.

One of my keenest memories of this is an agency presentation to AT&T. The clients were looking forward to seeing concepts to launch a loyalty program, and the agency was well prepared to show the first round of communications, which would use postal mail to reach the target audience. In the preceding days, account management, strategy, and production had met with creative to review and narrow down the concepts. The group selected three for presentation at the meeting. All three were on strategy for the brand and the campaign, had powerful graphics and messaging, and fulfilled all elements of the creative brief, including cost for production. What could go wrong? In the client conference room, the atmosphere was good. As the senior executive and account director leading the meeting, I was pleased. There was every reason to believe that we would get approval to proceed. At that point, the creative director suddenly stood up and announced that it was too soon to make a decision. He had a surprise, something more he wanted to show. (Whatever your professional stage, I'm sure you will agree that when your team is presenting, there should not be anything presented that is a surprise to anyone on your team.) So when the creative director went on to assert "You're going to love this new concept. I love it," I saw the meeting, the launch, and the business sliding away, as though the conference table had been tipped at a sharp angle. The surprise concept was a tiny envelope—a very tiny envelope. The designer hoped the diminutive size would "break the clutter" and get noticed in the mailbox.

"It's a joke, right?" asked one of the clients tactfully. Her colleagues were more pointed, expressing alarm that the agency would present a concept requiring special, costly print production and not meeting postal specifications for mailing. The meeting ended quickly. There were no further surprises: they did not approve any of the concepts that day. We kept the business, but not the creative director. In an experience like this meeting, one might want to defend the concept and argue for a way to overcome cost, production, or delivery barriers for a breakthrough design. The point of a book like this is that if a concept merits innovation, disruption, or change, you can and should be prepared to lead the discussion about why and how it would be feasible. The creative director was not prepared to do that. He hadn't considered any of those issues; his recommendation was based on subjectivity: "I love it." Subjectivity is not a compelling rationale for a business decision.

As Douglas Davis shows, the designer needs to understand more than design, to know all she or he can about the brand or organization, the target audience, the marketing strategy and goals, and the business itself. With his perspective as designer and teacher, he is able to bridge these elements.

In my own dual-career path, as a professor who became a marketer and then became a professor (again), I saw the value that my experience as an advertising executive brought to the classroom, and I saw that what is—unfortunately and inappropriately—termed "real-world experience" has even more value as social media continues to transform marketing. In the immediacy and transparency of virtual conversations and image-driven content, the marketer who has both theory and practical knowledge is prepared to evaluate the relative qualitative and quantitative cost and gain of a campaign or an Instagram posting.

Those in creative roles, especially, need to be prepared for the current and future marketplace. We don't know what the next wave of technology will bring to this field, but we do know there will be successive such waves, and they will demand more than big ideas and powerful design. In your work, you seek a competitive edge. A guidebook can be that edge, introducing you to methodology, terminology, and skills that can help you to achieve professional goals. The key to a good guidebook is the author's firsthand knowledge of the terrain. When Douglas was a student in my marketing-strategy classes, his ability to share his extensive design experience made him very popular with classmates, especially in courses where students developed sample campaigns. That ability also demonstrated that he would be a great teacher, as he proved to be when he joined the faculty after completing his graduate degree in marketing. It isn't possible for every designer to be a student in his classes. But this book is a highly readable and informative way to learn from him.

Marjorie Kalter, PhD
Former Director and Clinical Professor
Graduate Program in Integrated
Marketing, New York University

INTRODUCTION

My grandfather had a standing lunch date with a well-known conservative talk radio host. And that is how the host and I met, during lunchtime, standing in my grandparents' kitchen in South Carolina. I couldn't have been more than eight and by this time, I had heard my grandfather chuckle when referring to the things that ol' host would say for years. One day the host was ranting in a particularly offensive manner that registered as such in my still-forming second-grade brain. In my shock, I couldn't help but ask my grandfather, "Granddaddy, do you hear what he's saying, how can you listen to this!?" And without needing a moment to collect his thoughts, our family's wise gray-haired patriarch said with a smile, "I want to know what they think." Those seven words introduced my eight-year-old mind to the simple concept of seeking to understand the point of view opposite my own, and that's what this book is about.

At some point during my career, I realized that I lost creative battles because I was ignorant of the larger business or marketing considerations that informed aesthetics. I could write the design proposal, build the team, design or direct the executions, and pitch the ideas—yet I can remember times when none of this served me. Why? I didn't have the whole picture.

Then one day I stumbled into a strategy session. It was a completely new experience. The format was like brainstorming, but for a chess match. The discussion centered on trying to understand who the consumers were for this national sandwich shop we were pitching. What motivated them and why? How would our product fit within their lifestyle choices? Could we credibly position our product as a viable choice for them?

In that one meeting, where I had no formal strategy training to rely on, no concept of business, and no polished marketing vocabulary to add to the discussion, it all began to make sense. *This* was *that thing* that beat me. I *recognized it*, though I didn't *understand it*, and yet I did have a whole career of carrying out the result of meetings like this. I decided to become what I refer to as "a creative who understands business." So I applied to the Master's in Integrated Marketing program at New York University. The program was laser-focused on brand strategy, digital marketing, analytics, operations, and competitive strategy.

The result of adding left-brained strategic thinking to a right-brained creative problem solver equals clarity on the relationship between business objectives, marketing strategy, and the creative product.

Creative Strategy and the Business of Design came about as the result of my need to explore the words behind the pictures, understand the strategy behind the execution, and know the business objectives involved in the design process. You've also probably been impacted by this shift toward strategy in several ways, including a change in what your headhunters call you for, a broadening of the expectations the client has coming into a job, or the types of skills you've had to gain as a professional to remain relevant. A designer, copywriter, or freelance art director's success is now measured in metrics that include sales, downloads, page views, click-throughs, time on site, shares, likes, retweets, and ROI (return on investment). The results determine whether the effort was successful, creative, or worth trying again.

My goal in this book is to expose you to the peripheral marketing and business considerations that affect your job. And I hope that the book gives useful guidelines on *how* to think versus *what* to think. **Learning the language of business helped me win more business and get more design work, and I'd like to share what I've learned to help you do the same.**

Whether you are a creative focused on how beautiful the work can be, an account manager focused on pleasing the client, a new-business hunter focused on winning new accounts, or a marketer moving the needle on the metrics, creative problem-solving is a team sport with the same goal. So the question is: how do we begin with completely different points of view and responsibilities but end with a cohesive creative business solution? That's what this book will tackle. I'll present a translation from marketing-speak or business jargon into strategic tools that will help you or your team develop more relevant creative work. But that's just one side. I also invited some friends from the business side of the brain—marketers; brand, media, and communications strategists; writers; business people; planners; etc.—to detail their approach. Through them, you'll encounter the other people that we must work with to make it happen.

Let's start with what we weren't taught. As creative people, designers, art directors, writers, and those studying to become creative professionals, we were taught how to solve the creative portion of the client's problem. And we are good at it. So good, in fact, that clients can't help reason that since you've come through for them so many times with the execution—you must know strategy! The problem with this expectation is that it zeroes in on the very area that is outside the scope of what most of us were taught in design school: strategy. In D-school, we were taught to focus on the tactical parts of strategic decisions without even knowing what these strategic decisions entail. So when faced with a client's "tell me what to do, this or that" question, we may feel pressure to give a tactical this or that answer. Without any understanding of the marketing or business considerations that should shape this answer, any answer is at best incomplete. On the other side of the brain are the suits. As components of business, marketing, brand, or account management, many B-school programs are adept at imparting analytical thinking, competitive strategy, and marketing tactics. And they're good at it. Yet none of this teaches the skill of how to communicate in a way that gets the most out of the creative team. Stellar communication ability should be the common denominator among the creative and business players in the project, but this is where what we weren't taught makes the process harder. So here's what I'm proposing we do about it.

In Part I, A Designer Caught in the Headlights, I'll discuss the evolving role of a creative in a business and marketing context. You can think of this as the crash course in business and marketing for creatives.

In Part II, we will move into how to gather and organize all the relevant information you'll need to build creative solutions that are based on sound strategy, solve business objectives and lead the client.

In Part III, I'll give you what you need to develop and present your work. You'll find tips on collecting feedback and leading discussions in a constructive and meaningful way—*away* from the typical subjective comments such as "I don't like it."

We finish in Part IV, with the information you'll need to increase the value of your contribution to your clients and your career.

You'll also find a compilation of fourteen creative assignments from creative professionals that mirror recent requests their clients have asked them to solve. You can use these assignments to flex your new, strategy-based creative solutions to refresh your portfolio.

Over the course of my career, I've become increasingly focused on the thinking behind how things look. The inspiration behind the image. The words behind the pictures. I believe that if we can improve the communication within the creative process, we can improve the creative product. There is a big opportunity at the intersection of business strategy and creative execution, but leveraging it requires *understanding* what *they* think.

Thanks, Granddaddy.

A Designer Caught in the Headlights: Creative Business Solutions

1 Welcome to the Other Side of the Brain

Business Concepts Creatives Should Understand

It was only sixty minutes into my first statistics class—in the first week of my first semester at New York University—but I was already exceeding my median threshold for pain. Why was this a good idea again? I already had a Master's degree from Pratt Institute and a thriving career as a freelance art director who even taught an undergraduate class or two on the side. Nothing from the last hour was in any way familiar. What the hell did I just do? Each class I would fall further and further behind on the calculating and formulas and steps. Everything in me screamed *This is the wrong side of the brain!* I felt like Charlie Brown— everything I heard sounded like "wah-wah, wah-wah-wah-wah." I asked the professor for help. I asked my classmates for help. I failed the midterm. I paid a tutor for lessons twice a week and I wanted to quit before it all had really even begun. Though everyone else was competing for the highest score, I was only determined to make sure this class didn't defeat the whole purpose. On the final day, I slowly flipped my exam over and opened my eyes to see what I scored, and lo and behold, I was overjoyed to see that after my absolute best effort, I passed with a C. Academic probation never felt so good.

In a nutshell, I can say to you: the material in this book will sometimes make you feel like a creative person in a math class—it'll take some time and effort to grasp. Then, even after you want to grasp it, it takes some more time until it becomes second nature, so be patient with yourself. Trust me—it's worth it. Submerging myself into the world of "how they think" (a.k.a. the business world) slowly taught me why I lost the battles I did. The more integrated marketing classes I digested, the more I understood that an argument based on pure aesthetics was doomed unless it could be tied to accomplishing a business objective. This expedition to the other side of the brain helped me understand in detail what the difference is between art—a personal expression—and design/advertising—art with a commercial purpose.

Confused about what's strategy and what's execution? Think of it this way: When sitting down to play chess, your goal is to win by capturing the king. Thinking through the plan that details the pieces and process you'll use to do it is creating your strategy. The way you carry out that strategy, the actual moves themselves, or the tactics, are the execution. You'll hear people on the business or marketing side of things critique our ideas as "tactical" or "strategic" based on what's needed.

D-School Crashes B-School

After a year of kicking and screaming, I started to see the benefit of the way they think. Surprisingly, it increased the relevance/effectiveness of my creative work. In the Fred Nickols paper "Strategy IS Execution: What You Do Is What You Get," he states that "strategy as contemplated and strategy as realized are often two very different matters. Strategy as realized is the outcome of efforts to execute strategy as contemplated." It makes sense that if creative people are included at the table contemplating strategy from the outset, the more likely that strategy is to be realized when they execute. When I apply this thinking to our creative profession, it underscores my belief that injecting creativity into the beginning of a business discussion is the way to boost the success of the outcome. More importantly for the long term, it is the way to make the value of your relationship with the client invaluable. Relegating creativity to the execution or the end of solving a problem is an unfortunate misstep in a world of increased emphasis on aesthetics and design process. Our creative jobs are even more essential to business than in the past because of the way business is annexing design, as it previously integrated marketing. This concept isn't new: Thomas Watson Jr.'s comment in 1973 states that "good design is good business." However, the power and impact that design has had on business (as evidenced by visionaries like Steve Jobs) is reflected in the top business consulting firms like McKinsey&Compamy, advising in their article "Building a design-driven culture," that "[i]t's not enough to just sell a product or service— companies must truly engage with their customers." To bottom-line it, right-brained creativity is the spoonful of sugar that makes the business or marketing objectives (the left-brained component) palatable to the public.

I've watched clients' expectations evolve to the point that they now expect each person involved with their brand to be strategic. This includes the people tasked with building the customer-facing aspects of their communications—i.e., creative people, us. It doesn't matter that D-school doesn't focus heavily (if at all) on strategy or that B-school doesn't teach how to inspire creative people. Creative business solutions that have both rational and creative parts at their core are essential to differentiating you and your work from the pack.

Nickols' Strategy-Execution Matrix underscores the necessity of both parts of the brain working in harmony to even have a chance at creating something great. As our world becomes increasingly integrated, I'd argue that any approach that doesn't have equal parts right-brained creative problem-solving and left-brained strategic thinking will have a struggle making it through the internal process, much less making it to market.

	FLAWED	STRATEGY	SOUND
SOUND		"Shooting Yourself in the Foot"	"A Fighting Chance"
EXECUTION			
FLAWED		"Doomed from the Beginning"	"A Botched Job"

Chart courtesy of Fred Nickols.

Sound Execution + Flawed Strategy = Shooting Yourself in the Foot.
Sound Execution + Sound Strategy = A Fighting Chance.
Flawed Execution + Flawed Strategy = Doomed from the Beginning.
Flawed Execution + Sound Strategy = A Botched Job.

The Language of Business

If you've ever been in a meeting and everything that the client, account manager, or strategic planner said sounded like a foreign language, I understand. Business is spoken with the other side of the brain. Think of it as something like learning to draw with your nondominant hand—it will take a bit of getting used to.

Learning to speak the language is just the first part. In order to do what we're here to do, we've got to speak and *understand* the words being spoken around us. But, as you know, things get lost in translation. In this chapter, we'll start with the exposure to and translation of several key concepts. I'd like to help you connect with your clients and add value to your relationships by explaining how you can interpret the rational language of business while translating it into the emotional language of design.

If I had to cherry-pick the concepts most relevant to designers, writers, and art directors, it would be these. I'll give the gist of the concept first and then give scenarios that could help you incorporate these concepts into your approach to problem-solving.

Key Terms You Need to Know

The terms in this next section are not exhaustive, but are some of the usual suspects. If you want to impress a dinner date, this is what you've been doing at work all these years. I've organized this section in order from what you may encounter the most in your everyday job to the higher-level concepts you may face as you become more seasoned. The list ends with a framework to organize all this in a way that will help you create from it.

A key point: these terms are always relative. Meaning, the term used might vary from company to company or situation to situation—it depends on the person using it, the culture of the agency, and so on. Use the context you see the term in to help guide you toward what's being referenced. If necessary, ask for clarification!

Understanding these key business concepts will allow you to:

▸ Build your creative concepts on a solid strategic understanding.

▸ Ask relevant questions that help fill in the blanks when information is vague or incomplete.

▸ Win new and grow existing business relationships.

When you're really able to use these terms correctly, eyebrows will raise.

[INSIGHT]

WHAT IS IT?

In this context, an insight is the gold that we mine from company data, target-market research, or brand history to inspire our creative concepts. Insights are a set of conclusions rooted in truth that you can think of as distilled inspiration. When looking at data on sales or behaviors, questions like these can lead to insights:

▸ What is it telling us about the people we are observing and the decisions they make?

▸ Does the data point to an underlying truth about the values of the people we are observing?

▸ Does the data contradict what we assume to be true or confirm something we didn't even know was there? If so, how could we quantify and articulate that information on a broader scale?

An insight will help present something widely known from a new angle or help frame new information in an interesting way. When pitching a new idea, often an insight will accompany an observation and together gives us the ability to state the implications from the information collected.

Here's an example of an observation and insight that could be inspired from research. Let's say you're working with the Gotham Writers Workshop.

Observation: In Malcolm Gladwell's book *Outliers*, he asserts that it takes at least 10,000 hours practice to master something.

Insight: If you look at that from the beginning writer's perspective, someone just starting out will need to overcome a great deal of insecurity, a mountain of rewrites, and the overall temptation to quit.

The process of developing an insight is a difficult two-part procedure that requires first the observation of an existing truth and then the crafting of the conclusion or conclusions that follow. From there, the observation and resulting insight can inspire multiple concepts and even more executions. Information collected + data interpreted = insights that inspire concepts that inspire executions.

WHY IS IT IMPORTANT?

Strong insights inspired by data or research inspire strong concepts. Strong concepts inspire relevant and compelling creative work. Relevant and compelling creative work wins clients and new business. Therefore here's a concept and resulting execution that could be inspired by the insight about Gladwell's observation:

Concept: Behind every great speech, book, or script are a ton of revisions, and though people are familiar with the finished versions of the I have a dream speech, the novel *To Kill a Mockingbird*, or the screenplay for *The Dark Knight*, new writers (our target) are less familiar with the process it takes to get to great.

Execution: Introduce new writers to the development process by showing the potential phases well-known lines went through to get to what we all know and recognize. Calls to action (CTAs) will correspond with the type of work being edited and the relevant Gotham class.

WHAT JOB TITLE/ROLE IS CONCERNED WITH THIS?

Creative strategists, writers, creative directors, art directors, and designers: whoever is tasked with briefing the creative team or inspiring them through writing the creative brief should be versed in extracting informed insights. If you are developing ideas of any kind, it's your job to look for insights that inspire the work. Depending on the culture of your organization, the person determining insights could be a more senior person or a strategist, but it's good for everyone to understand how to work from them.

FOR MORE ON THE SUBJECT

Read *Hey, Whipple, Squeeze This: The Classic Guide to Creating Great Ads* by Luke Sullivan with Sam Bennett.

Self-actualization

Esteem

Love/Belonging

Safety

Physiological

Morality,
creativity,
spontaneity,
problem solving,
lack of prejudice,
acceptance of facts

Self-esteem, confidence,
achievement, respect of others

Friendship, family, sexual intimacy

Security of body, of employment, of resources,
of morality, of family, of health, of property

Breathing, food, water, sex, sleep, homeostasis, excretion

WHAT IS IT?

Maslow's hierarchy of needs is a theory that attempts to explain the psychology of curiosity and human development. It was proposed by Abraham Maslow in his paper "A Theory of Human Motivation," which was published in 1943 in *Psychological Review*. You may be thinking, "Why are we talking about this"—hold your horses. Marketing and business programs mention Maslow's hierarchy of needs when delving into consumer behavior. Abraham Maslow identified what he saw as five stages of human needs. As you can see in the figure, at the most basic level, or the bottom, are the needs that sustain life itself. These items include breathing, food, and water and are labeled

physiological needs. Once those needs are taken care of, someone typically would be free to seek safety. After that comes the relational needs of belonging and love. Status or esteem needs follow, and last, at the top, is the abstract need for self-actualization.

How do these needs translate into consumer behavior? Have you ever considered that the person buying the whitening toothpaste may really be out to brush away self-consciousness? Or that the guy purchasing the hair regrowth product may really want to regrow his confidence? A whiter smile or a fuller head of hair is what a product may promise on the surface, but the deeper, underlying meaning that these things represent in the mind of the consumer is what successful creative messaging should speak to.

WHY IS THIS IMPORTANT?

Understanding the underlying need behind a purchase would help us determine how to incorporate it into the creative approach. Anyone using the hierarchy could incorporate any underlying insights into a creative brief, creative concept, or pitch setup. This makes for a much more compelling brief, concept, or story. For example, if you're designing a campaign for a tooth whitener, you could use Maslow's hierarchy to help you draw conclusions from the research on a target's reason behind wanting whiter teeth. Look at the functional aspects of the product as a means to an end that is below the surface (Love/belonging or Esteem). From there, your concept could utilize words and pictures that either illustrate the confidence you'll get as a result of using the toothpaste or show life without it.

WHAT JOB TITLE/ROLE IS CONCERNED WITH THIS?

Writers, creative directors, art directors, and designers can use this hierarchy as a way to uncover what the product could really mean to the purchaser. Adding needs to a creative brief will inspire designers on a conceptual level.

FOR MORE ON THE SUBJECT

Read: *Relevance: The Power to Change Minds and Behavior and Stay Ahead of the Competition* by Andrea Coville.

[SEGMENTATION]

WHAT IS IT?

"Segmenting" refers to dividing your target into groups based on such characteristics as:

▸ Demographics

▸ The target's life stage

▸ Psychographics (the study of a target's interests, attitudes, and opinions)

▸ The behaviors and actions a target takes

Looking at these categories will enable you to speak specifically to the individuals via concepts, media, copy, and design of the marketing message. For example, you wouldn't talk with a seven-year-old girl who only spoke French, a thirty-eight-year-old businessman, and a seventy-two-year-old grandfather in the same way. Therefore, you shouldn't "speak" to them the same way in your advertising, design, or copy either. What they have in common is that they all like Coke Classic—however, because of their various life stages, media consumption, and language needs, you would need to develop messaging tailored to them in order to reach them.

WHY IS THIS IMPORTANT?

Segmentation is important because it allows you to drill down to what is relevant to the individuals—making your message suit each target, instead of speaking the same way to, say, men and women between the ages of 7 and 72.

Creative directors, senior designers, and writers will be concerned with segmentation. Anyone on a pitch team or looking for new business will need to understand segmentation and its strategic relevance to creative execution.

FOR MORE ON THE SUBJECT
Read *Aaker on Branding: 20 Principles That Drive Success* by David A. Aaker.

[DIFFERENTIATION]

WHAT IS IT?
Differentiation is simply what makes something different from something else in the same category. Say you're walking down the sugar aisle in the grocery store and you need a five-pound bag. There are several well-known national brands you could choose, as well as the store brand. If you believe that all sugar is created equal, then there is no differentiation in the mind of the consumer, only a commodity. When this is the case, the consumer will choose on the basis of the lowest price.

WHY IS IT IMPORTANT?
Differentiation is important because it sets one product (or designer, for that matter) apart from another. This differentiation can be achieved with a unique package design or strong visual brand that calls attention to one product versus another. It could be achieved through, for example, a strong brand heritage or story that is leveraged and

reminds the consumer of his or her mother's choice of sugar. Or it could be achieved on the basis of how the sugar is produced or grown that makes it eco-friendly or healthier. When consumers see the product as much more than "ordinary" sugar, they in theory are willing to pay more and remain loyal to the brand.

**WHAT JOB TITLE/ROLE IS
CONCERNED WITH THIS?**
Designers, art directors, copywriters, and creative directors are all a part of activating or bringing to life the story of how this product is different than that product. It is our job to tell the story of that differentiating feature so that customers not only know the difference, but are willing to pay more for it (because, say, they prefer and choose organic brown sugar).

FOR MORE ON THE SUBJECT
Read *Blue Ocean Strategy, Expanded Edition: How to Create Uncontested Market Space and Make the Competition Irrelevant* by W. Chan Kim and Renée Mauborgne.

[FEATURES AND BENEFITS]

WHAT ARE THEY?
In the simplest terms, *features* of a brand, product, or service are tangible, like the physical features of a person. Some examples include:

- ▸ How fast the processor is on a Google Chromebook with an Intel processor

- The unique ball on a high-end Dyson vacuum cleaner
- The white-glove furniture delivery service from Restoration Hardware

These are the tangible things that make up what a product is and will be shown or listed in some way on the creative execution or in the copy.

The *benefits* of these individual features are intangible benefits to the consumer:

- The benefit to the consumer with the Chromebook is the ability to be more productive because of multitasking (processing speed enables productivity)
- Depending on your perspective, the benefit to the consumer with the Dyson could be no more excuses for avoiding large family gatherings because of the ease of cleanup due to the increased maneuverability (the ball enables easy cleanup)
- The benefit to the consumer using the white glove service of Restoration Hardware is knowing how easy it is to return or replace at no additional cost if you don't like the furniture when you get it home (white-glove furniture delivery)

WHY IS THIS IMPORTANT?

These features and benefits allow us to write headlines, write copy, and design campaigns compelling to the target by ensuring that we are defining the utility of the product in terms that demonstrate what's in it for the consumer. These benefits can express themselves in the scenario being shown in the visual or written portion of the work being described in the headlines or body copy.

WHAT JOB TITLE/ROLE IS CONCERNED WITH THIS?

Writers, designers, art directors, and creative directors will find this useful when developing concepts to execute. For example, headlines can be feature statements or benefit statements. Visual concepts can be developed around demonstrating a particular scenario that shows the absence of a particular benefit to highlight having it.

FOR MORE ON THE SUBJECT

Read *Words that Sell: More than 6,000 Entries to Help You Promote Your Products, Services, and Ideas* by Richard Bayan.

[THE PURCHASE FUNNEL]

Awareness
Mass, OOH, TV, Radio, Print

Research
Digital, POS, Mobile, DR: Print, TV

Engagement
Digital, POS

Convert
Digital, POS, Mobile, Print (DM)

Post Purchase
Digital, Mobile, Print (DM), WOM

Advocacy
Digital, WOM

WHAT IS IT?

The purchase funnel is a way to understand the stages a customer goes through on the way to a purchase, and then to becoming loyal to a brand or product. The concept is really a business-y way to explain the process of buying something, beginning with making you aware that it exists. After you know that it exists, you may want to read up on it and some others like it to determine which one is right for you based on its features. You might also dive into online reviews, ask people who already have one if they like it, or head to the store to try it yourself. After gathering enough information and making a selection, you cough up the cash and make the transition from prospect to proud owner. Once it's yours, you may need help from the manufacturer to take care of it or get it serviced, and now you'll rate how well they are doing in online reviews. Based on the overall experience, you'll either recommend it to others or begin the process anew because you were unhappy with it or have a different need based on how your life has evolved.

Think back to your decision-making process when you bought your first iPhone. You knew you wanted it; the questions were what color and how many gigs. Or, remember when you bought your first MacBook. Since we are creatives, there was no internal debate, only a decision to go with the retina screen and solid-state drive or opt for the largest storage capacity. Pretty simple, right?

Well, think of all the people who don't automatically go for Apple products. Those people have a much harder time making these decisions, because they also consider many other brands that can meet their needs: e.g., Samsung, Nokia, Google or HP, Microsoft, Lenovo. Then they must research these options and compare each of them to determine which features best serve their needs. Then at some point they decide and purchase. If they are satisfied with their purchase, they may become "advocates"—recommending the same choice to friends and family.

WHY IS THIS IMPORTANT?

Understanding these points along the consumer's journey will help us recommend the correct format and media channels based on the decisions the consumer needs to make in each stage. Let's say Lenovo (which acquired IBM's personal computer division in 2005) has a new laptop. In order for the public to consider it, they would first need a brand campaign to make the public aware of the new name the new offering comes from. Once aware of this choice, it would be helpful for consumers to have a website they could visit to learn about all the features and benefits of the product. Since the public may be comparing on their mobile devices, this website design would need to work in any channel the consumer is researching in. When the choice is made to purchase, the website would need e-commerce capabilities in case the consumer wanted to buy.

After the purchase, the brand would do well to make it easy to engage with the customer's friends in various ways, through social media or making a support site easily accessible. This will give the new customer a sense that the brand is supporting his or her purchase by standing behind the product and therefore give something positive to tweet or post about in social media (and the opposite is true if the experience or product fails to live up to what was advertised). Some view this concept as old, and yes, the funnel concept was developed before social media, digital natives, or smartphones. The customer journey and the ability to track it (if crafted right) could tend to offer more specific behavioral insights that acknowledge the point of entry according to behavior versus assuming it would be from traditional mass-media channels that yield large audiences. Regardless of the tool you or your organization uses, it is important to understand the stages in order to craft messaging that achieves the objectives in each stage.

WHAT JOB TITLE/ROLE IS CONCERNED WITH THIS?

Creative directors, freelance designers, and writers who are making strategy recommendations are likely to use the purchase funnel concept. This tool can be used to determine what tangible design deliverables, written offers, or calls to action will be needed in the creative work.

FOR MORE ON THE SUBJECT
Read *Targeted: How Technology Is Revolutionizing Advertising and the Way Companies Reach Consumers* by Mike Smith.

[MARKETING ALLOWABLE]

WHAT IS IT?

A marketing allowable is the amount of money a brand has determined it can spend on a new customer. Ever wonder why those timeshare sellers offer to give you all that free stuff in exchange for your time? It's because they've calculated that the free surf-and-turf dinner at the upscale restaurant, the jet ski voucher for two, and the glass-bottom boat tour are all well within what they stand to gain should you sign on the dotted line. In fact, the marketing folks have already subtracted it from the overall amount of profit they will make over the lifetime value or money they'll gain from their relationship with you. So in other words, free shipping, the free tote bag with purchase, and the free steak and lobster are, you guessed it—not free. The higher the item's price, the higher marketing allowable in the budget, and the more expensive the items offered to get your attention.

WHY IS IT IMPORTANT?

Though I don't want to give you nightmares by bringing up the numbers, knowing what they are in some situations will give you an understanding of what you have to spend on gifts to sweeten the pot. To sum it up, a marketing allowable is a part of a broader acquisition initiative designed to turn leads or prospects into new customers. If you work in promotions, often you'll need to gain your target's attention by building a design idea around a premium. An HGTV promotion for a house could include a welcome to the neighborhood basket with an antique key inside the brochure. In this example, the basket, the fruit, the key, and the printing for the brochure would all need to be within the allowable. The ideas for the offer need to be compelling so as to attract the most responses, and the profit gained from each successful purchase should more than cover what it cost to produce. As new platforms emerge and digital behavior evolves, new-customer-acquisition costs change.

WHAT JOB TITLE/ROLE IS CONCERNED WITH THIS?

Marketing allowables are most relevant for freelancers, art directors, and designers working in promotions for various media properties, or designers embedded with marketing departments. This concept is essential when pitching promotional design concepts in a data-driven marketing context.

FOR MORE ON THE SUBJECT
Read *Digilogue: How to Win the Digital Minds and Analogue Hearts of Tomorrow's Customer* by Anders Sorman-Nilsson.

[METRIC]

WHAT IS IT?

Peter Drucker, the writer, professor, and management consultant *BusinessWeek* dubbed "the man who invented management," is quoted as saying, "If you can't measure it, you can't improve it." Metrics are points of information that businesses or brands use to determine how well they are doing with the "numbers"—such as reducing cost, increasing response rate to an ad, or setting a sales benchmark to beat. The success of a business is determined through metrics that include:

▸ time on website

▸ response rate

▸ click-through rate (CTR)

▸ cost per thousand (CPM, the cost of 1,000 "impressions" in advertising)

▸ conversion rate

▸ open rate

▸ number of unsubscribes, likes, retweets, and referrals

▸ recency of purchase

▸ frequency of purchase

▸ monetary value (the previous three are RFM)

▸ average order value of customers (AOV)

With these measures, you can better manage common key objectives of increasing the time on site, reducing the number of unsubscribes, and increasing monetary value of orders through creative campaigns.

WHY IS IT IMPORTANT?

When you understand what a business or brand is trying to accomplish, you can propose solutions that answer the business problem with creativity. Since each organization is different, creatives may or may not have access to these metrics, but a smart creative director or informed designer can make these assumptions in order to focus on them in the work. For instance:

▸ If your assignment is to design a digital ad campaign, you can assume that the goal is to drive as much traffic as possible somewhere.

▸ If you are designing packaging for a product, then the number of sales is being measured.

▸ If you are designing signage or exhibition materials for an event, the number of people who will visit the booth is important to keep track of.

Knowing what is being measured allows you to do the detective work of finding out more about where the campaign will be seen, where the ads click through to, what other products your packaging will be seen with, and so on. With this information, you can look for insights that differentiate your concepts relative to competitors or that leverage the context they will be seen in to achieve the goals or the metrics you aim to measure.

Creative directors and everyone involved in developing creative business solutions will work with metrics.

FOR MORE ON THE SUBJECT

Read *The New Rules of Marketing & PR: How to Use Social Media, Online Video, Mobile Applications, Blogs, News Releases, and Viral Marketing to Reach Buyers Directly* by David Meerman Scott.

[THE BRAND LADDER]

WHAT IS IT?

This methodology originated at Procter & Gamble in the 1960s and has been used at agencies such as WPP's Y&R to build brands. Think of a brand ladder as the foundation of a house because it's built from the ground up:

1. First, you start with the **features** (or attributes of a brand) that express the tangible aspects of what a brand is.

2. Next, you layer on top of the features the corresponding **benefits** to the target consumer.

3. On top of those benefits, you identify and list the **values** the target uses to make decisions about whatever it is that your brand is selling.

4. Lastly, you use each of these three pieces to create a "positioning statement" that was developed from the content below it—what's known as "laddering up."

WHY IS THIS IMPORTANT?

This is a tool that helps connect the brand and the target. Using this ladder technique, a designer can ensure that he or she is creating in the voice of the brand within what is relevant to the target. With a sound brand ladder connecting the brand and target, creative people can take risks that are rooted firmly in relevance.

**WHAT JOB TITLE/ROLE IS
CONCERNED WITH THIS?**

Creative directors, senior designers, and writers will use the brand ladder. Anyone on a pitch team or looking for new business will need to understand these elements because of their strategic relevance to creative execution.

FOR MORE ON THE SUBJECT

Read *Understanding Consumer Decision Making: The Means-End Approach to Marketing and Advertising Strategy* by Thomas J. Reynolds and Jerry C. Olson.

[THE POSITIONING STATEMENT]

WHAT IS IT?

This tool is a succinct articulation of the target, brand, business category, point of difference (see Chapter 9 for more information), and "reason to believe" associated with a product or service. (I'm simplifying this for our discussion— these consumer-behavior concepts are rigorous and in-depth research tools and are actually far more complicated.)

I use the following framework for crafting a positioning statement after doing the research needed to fill in the blanks: "For (target), (brand or product) is the (category) that delivers (benefit/ point of difference) because only (brand name) is (reason to believe based on a tangible attribute or feature)."

Whether you're developing a brand from scratch or repositioning a brand, you must have a crystal-clear understanding of the people you are targeting because the objective is to "position" the brand in their minds. In order to do that, it is essential to zero in on what it is that makes your product a perfect match for the consumer and vice versa. Once you as a designer, art director, copywriter, or creative services manager have a sense of the specifics of a project from a client meeting, strategic planner, or your own research, it may be helpful to take a stab at developing the brand positioning statement.

WHY IS THIS IMPORTANT?

This statement will allow clarity in direction by precisely defining the chemistry between the brand and target. Clarity in articulation means less time wasted in the creative conceptualization and execution phases. It also allows the thread of strategy to help inspire and justify the creative executions proposed. Note that you cannot create a sound positioning statement without building it from the ground up in a brand ladder.

WHAT JOB TITLE/ROLE IS CONCERNED WITH THIS?

Creative directors, senior designers, and writers will rely on positioning statements. Anyone on a pitch team or who is trying to get new business will need to understand these elements because of their strategic relevance to creative execution.

FOR MORE ON THE SUBJECT

Read *Positioning: The Battle for Your Mind* by Al Ries and Jack Trout.

[BRAND ACTIVATION]

WHAT IS IT?

Brand activation is the tangible experience a consumer has as a result of the communications they encounter from that brand. As brands communicate their values to consumers through promises, creative people are charged with bringing these promises to life through experiences we develop on behalf of these brands. With that, we "activate," or build, a branded experience through an app, event, website, identity, package, point of purchase display, pop-up store concept, or advertising campaign. This activation can be as simple as building an event around an organization's tagline or developing creative concepts that focus on demonstrating a distinguishing feature of a product.

Think BMW's Performance Driving School, where they teach you to handle their Ultimate Driving Machines like a pro, or an *American Gladiator*-styled event called a Gentleman's Disagreement where contestants wear Haggar casual clothing, a brand that boasts unbreakable buttons and unbustable seams.

WHY IS IT IMPORTANT?

Creative people are an invaluable part of the communications that bring brands to life. Understanding what a brand stands for and the intended target's profile helps to develop experiences that are on brand, on strategy, and on message. The moment of truth comes when customers experience the product itself and then determine whether what was advertised matches up with the experience. We've all been disappointed or felt lied to when we've paid for products that haven't performed as advertised. If the product itself falls short, no amount of great design or advertising can fix that (as in the case of the recent Volkswagen diesel emissions scandal). On the other end of the spectrum, we've all been delighted when a product exceeds expectations and performs well beyond what was advertised (like the cracked iPhone that still works perfectly though you drop it like you hate it). Some scenarios exist where the product is average but the creative idea, design, or packaging is what's memorable. It is clear that the creative team has done their job when the advertising and experience match.

WHAT JOB TITLE/ROLE IS CONCERNED WITH THIS?

Creative directors and everyone involved in developing creative business solutions will pay a lot of attention to brand activation strategies.

FOR MORE ON THE SUBJECT

Read *How 30 Great Ads Were Made: From Idea to Campaign* by Eliza Williams.

[SCENARIO ANALYSIS]

WHAT IS IT?

Scenario analysis is a way to anticipate and think through the impact of each option we recommend to our client. In our context, it allows the designer to create options based on a feature of the product or aspect of competition in the business category and present it with the risks and potential rewards of going with each option.

For example, as designers, we often generate what seems like hundreds of sketches before selecting three options to present our clients. If we are freelancing, it's usually one job, three options for one price. The job could range from an app interface to a brand identity, but three options with an agreed-upon number of revisions is usually the case. At best, these options are not just variations of the same thing, they are Rhinoceros, Rainbow, and Rhombus—in other words, completely different ways to solve the same problem:

- The Rhinoceros option may have been inspired by the strength of the product we are creating for.

- The Rainbow option may have come from the colors available or the variety of uses for the product.

- The unique shape of the product may differentiate it from the competitors and may have inspired the Rhombus option.

WHY IS IT IMPORTANT?

Scenario analysis is important because if your client is a market leader on the basis of the strength of their product, but sales are suggesting that consumers are also valuing aesthetics nowadays, you could advise on the risks and rewards of going with Rhombus over Rhinoceros. I've found in my career that though everyone has an opinion, clients will pay for your analysis. It's also important to be able to say with authority that you are recommending these options because the client needs them and not because you are trying to sell them something. As the expert, you make the recommendations but scenario analysis allows the client to make informed decisions.

WHAT JOB TITLE/ROLE IS CONCERNED WITH THIS?

Scenario analysis is relevant to freelance designers, creative directors, or whoever is presenting and justifying the work during a pitch or presentation.

FOR MORE ON THE SUBJECT
Read *Developing Business Strategies* by David A. Aaker.

[CREATIVE STRATEGY FRAMEWORK]

WHAT IS IT?

In my experience, creatives often either get incomplete information or are bombarded with too much information. I found it difficult to do my creative job in both cases: when I had to work to fill in the gaps or to sift through the irrelevant parts of the information overload. So I created this simple tool for organizing and extracting insights called the "creative strategy framework."

The framework uses four columns to help you organize the elements involved in developing creative work and focus on seeing the threads that exist between creativity and strategy:

1. Target

2. Facts (on the brand, product, or service)

3. Feature/Benefit

4. Message or Objective (depending on the priority)

We'll learn much more about this framework in Chapters 6 and 7.

The most practical way I've used this tool is in a kickoff meeting, when we are sitting with the client to learn about the project. Often, we must play detective in our research because the briefing process and people involved only give us pieces of the puzzle we are being tasked with solving. Having the chart in front of you to organize your notes helps begin the process of developing relevant solutions that are on brand, on strategy, and on message. You'll also be able to tell if you're missing information, so you can ask for it right at the meeting.

This tool is flexible because the resulting strategic threads can be used to inspire creative work—for example, in writing a creative brief or in developing creative concepts.

WHAT JOB TITLE/ROLE IS CONCERNED WITH THIS?

Creative strategist, writers, creative directors, art directors, and designers could find value in this framework in their process. Whoever is tasked with gathering information, briefing the creative team, or inspiring the team through writing the creative brief should be versed in extracting informed insights. This tool can help.

FOR MORE ON THE SUBJECT

Visit *www.mydesignshop.com/creative-strategy-framework-design-tutorial* for an in-depth tutorial.

Turning Words Into Inspiration

Now that you've been exposed to the words behind the pictures or the strategy behind the execution, it's time to think about how you can apply these concepts in your day-to-day creative work. As you go through this book, you'll see the greatest results if you read with the intention to reapply the concepts in some way immediately. To help you do that, think about which concepts, definitions, or tools in this recap are most relevant to your current job, project, or client work. As you do that, remember:

▸ These terms might be called something slightly different in certain companies.

▸ Feel free to refer back to this chapter as often as you need to.

▸ Practice using the terms so you become more comfortable with them.

2 Emerging from the Cocoon

The Benefits of a Strategic Approach

I got a call one day while sitting in my apartment in Manhattan. A longtime marketer in the business who awarded me a scholarship while I was at NYU had an assistant who was on the other line. She said, "I'm now a marketing manager for a small but growing employee staffing company and we need a new positioning and identity materials to update our offering. I'd love to get your recommendation on any design firms we could consider to send our request for proposal."

"Absolutely!" I said, as I rattled off the top-tier design and branding firms known around the world but based in New York (Carbone Smolan, Pentagram, Wolff Olins, Landor, Interbrand, FutureBrand, Chermayeff & Geismar). I was completely confident that any one of these could exceed all expectations. I was positive that for a truckload of money, my old friend would be buying the best work the industry had to offer. After finishing my list and just before hanging up the phone, I heard "—and feel free to throw your hat in the ring; I know you do the work we need as well."

At that point it occurred to me that the award from years ago flagged me as both a contact in New York and a credible professional in the business. After hanging up the phone, my first boss in advertising immediately popped into my head. We had kept in touch over the years. I had long since moved on from that first job, but I never forgot the work we did under his direction and still admired him for the way he approached advertising through design. I realized it would be a great time to partner with him and the usual talent suspects in his orbit once again. We'd all worked together and enjoyed the freedom and risks we could take together. So I made the call, and between the two of us, we had the creative and conceptual skills needed to credibly throw our hats in the ring.

Our motley crew pulled together a capabilities presentation of relevant case studies, and built a team of people who would work on the business should we win. The client flew up and we pitched in a small rented office in Chelsea. After one more pitch we were awarded the work. Winning the business couldn't have gone better. Former co-workers. Talent who had worked on numerous well-known global accounts. Complete confidence in our ability to create a beautiful new identity the client asked for . . . if only we could agree on what the strategic parts were.

Disagreeing That We Agree: Tactical versus Strategic

Our discord was one that I imagine many a creative team has when trying to get on the same page about strategy. In this case, we weren't in agreement on what strategy actually was. The client asked for "positioning" and some on the team thought that writing a tagline would be sufficient to satisfy this part of the request. However, a positioning is, by definition, a *strategic* exercise and therefore should never be customer-facing. It is a part of what I've been calling "the words behind the pictures" or the "strategy behind the execution."

This disagreement made the process of arriving at either a specific positioning or a broad strategy a struggle.

On one hand, the veterans I was working with had been in the business much longer than I had. Their experience building well-known brands by conceptualizing and designing their well-known campaigns was why I wanted to partner with them in the first place. I learned quite a bit about being a creative by working with them and watching them present. I had deep respect for the way they approached the work from a creative perspective. And that is what they were doing now— taking an execution-oriented approach, which consisted of creating a tagline and building a campaign around it.

THE BENEFITS OF BUILDING ON STRATEGY

The veterans' approach had worked for them in the past, but at this point, I knew that the business required *more*

from us. I had a deep understanding of marketing strategy, and though I was the "digital guy" on the team, I had valid opinions on how and why we should arrive at the overall strategic foundation. To build a campaign based on strategy, we needed to get deeper into the category to understand the landscape, including the competition and their strategic positions. From there, we could find a white-space opportunity or point of difference to build our positioning around. Next, we'd crystalize our insight into a client-facing positioning statement that would inspire all consumer-facing elements (including the tagline).

This process creates clarity on managing the brand. It would then inspire the work we were hired to do, and also help us advise the client on what they shouldn't do in the future. With a strong strategic foundation, the brand could be managed after our project and this would provide guideposts for anyone who came after us to understand what was and what was not conducive to strengthening the brand.

THE DRAWBACKS OF CREATING WITHOUT STRATEGY

Don't get me wrong; great campaign concepts have been made by simply writing a tagline or sentence that helps focus or sum up what the campaign is about. On this surface level, tactical creativity aligns with the brand and those are essentially the only words behind the pictures. What you see is what you get. Using this method, the creative team is united about what they think works creatively and strategically.

However, I've found that it also makes for two big problems:

1. First, it leaves the creatives having to fight everyone else on the pitch team to keep them out of the work. At this point, it is us, the creative group, against everybody else on the internal team. From the creativity standpoint, this is the perfect solution because we creatives have the power. The drawbacks to this approach are that it could undermine the overall firm and defeat the purpose of having business or strategic expertise available. Big, creative personalities often get their way.

2. This dynamic leads to a perpetually subjective scenario built on trusting individuals for trust's sake. As in, "Just trust me!" There are no arguments based in fact; it's just throwing weight around. At that point, there might as well be an announcer with a microphone proclaiming, "Let the combative tension-filled interactions and subjective disagreements commence!" You can smell fear in the air in every meeting when everyone is being told essentially to stay in their lane. Egos are now involved because the focus is on defending my idea versus meeting the client request in an objective and strategic way. At worst these discussions create internal factions based on job function where rank is pulled and posturing is practiced. *I like the blue logo! I like the red!* In this type of environment, the client's request that got us into the room is buried under the preferences in the room.

Furthermore, because the execution-oriented solution was developed without sound strategic roots, the team with this approach presents the client with two choices:

1. Stay now and leave later. Why? The client who asks for a tactical element (like a tagline) is trying to accomplish a strategic goal even if they don't know it yet. When that tactical element fails to achieve that strategic goal, the conclusion is that your work is at fault.

or

2. Leave now for a more strategic partner. Strategy is why the client left whoever had their business before they searched for your firm, so strategy is a large part of the reason you'll lose it.

If the client chooses to "stay now," and go with that subjectivity for the short term, it's usually on the strength of the creative idea, without well-reasoned rules on managing their brand consistently going forward. This approach produces a less cohesive overall brand, because its premise was based on the opinion of someone inside the creative team and *not the target*. What happens if that person leaves, is fired, or makes a different decision concerning what they like? If you've ever wondered why a new communication from a brand didn't sound familiar in tone or look as if it belonged to the brand in some way, it could be the result of not having a sound strategic foundation.

This choice also leaves the account vulnerable to the client's whims and subjectivity on matters that they should leave up to the creative team. At this point, each interaction is as fun as a trip to the dentist's office to remove yet another molar. In the end, the client's trust in the creative's subjective opinion only lasts so long, because if the client goals and metrics weren't reached, they blame you.

To put it another way, it's like the difference between going with the cellular data plan that sounds good on a commercial versus calling the phone company, asking them to look at your data usage for the last six months, and deciding based on what you actually use. Without a *real* strategic process, the "strategy" consists of why certain words, typefaces, or colors were selected—and though all of these tangible aspects of a brand are important, they aren't a strategic foundation.

Emerging from the Cocoon

After learning the language of business, I had a more complete understanding of how to develop positioning based on research. This new perspective made it impossible for me to justify creative recommendations that were not rooted in strategy. As a result, I found it difficult to fit into a rigid execution-only role because my approach now required an insight inspired from research, and when the research was weak or nonexistent, I challenged it.

In the case of my opening story, though the client was happy with the design and application, we only solved 50 percent of the brief because of the tactical impulse to create. As a result, we provided short-term tactical decisions instead of a sound strategic foundation that enables long-term brand management. Despite my objections and history with this rockstar creative team, ultimately our team didn't understand the value of arriving at a back-end strategy before creating the front-end solutions. As a result, it is my opinion that we failed to offer a long-term positioning that the client could use to manage their brand into the future. You may experience this impulse in your teams. It expresses itself in various ways, such as a failure to listen to each other or an unwillingness to consider other approaches to the problem. Sure, you can encounter stubborn personalities on any team, but without an objective strategic approach based on research, you won't be able to move the conversation toward a constructive discussion about the client objectives. People might still get emotional about what they like, but you have a way out of difficult conversations: facts. If you don't have facts and strategy behind you, eventually it becomes clear that you're just arguing for a creative *idea*, not a *creative business solution*.

The Long-Term Advantages of the Strategic Approach

As you're learning, approaching a creative job from a strategic standpoint is much more effective. Yes, it takes longer in terms of up-front research, but it yields better results—both for the immediate campaign and for future endeavors. Consider the following situations, and notice the difference between the tactical (execution-based) approach and the strategic one:

Tactical: Jumping into the ocean to learn how to swim.
Strategic: Taking swimming lessons.

Tactical: Eating all the M&M's because they taste great.
Strategic: Eating things your head knows are good for your mouth.

Tactical: Letting the deadline dictate your approach to the problem.
Strategic: Budgeting your time thoughtfully to properly explore the complete context of a problem so as to see its root cause and factoring that into the solution.

Tactical: Taking a cough suppressant for weeks.
Strategic: Testing for pneumonia.

Clearly, the strategic approach is always the better one for long-term success.

Turning Words Into Inspiration

As a creative, I believe that we should lead the client when building relationships between the brand and its target customers.

Think of the project you are working on currently, then try this exercise:

1. Try to identify areas where there is confusion or a lack of clarity on the strategic way forward.

2. Without blame, try to put your finger on the top two or three reasons why. If it will help, label them with headers such as Process, Communication, or Strategy.

3. After articulating the reasons, formulate a solution for each, in no more than two or three sentences each.

4. Lastly, add the projected impact or benefit of that solution on your creative process, product or communication. You may need a draft or two to present your point of view in the most objective language possible.

Now you are ready to identify the person most likely to be receptive to hearing your thoughts and the most opportune time to present them. Who knows—you may get fired but you may also get a chance to take the lead on implementing these solutions.

3 What They Say versus What We Hear

Translating Client Requests

Back in January 2015 I received a very kind invitation to give a keynote address in St. Petersburg, Russia, at an Art and Branding conference. I was one of four international speakers (and the only American) invited to share the stage with the top Russian experts in branding. My first thought was, "Yeah, right, who knows my work in Russia? This is fake." But it turned out that it was a legit invite from a reputable organization.

Fast forward. I'm on stage and the discussion begins in Russian, so I can't understand anything. My translator is furiously scribbling down notes and every so often whispers a summary of what is being discussed in my ear. I answer a few questions, with well-reasoned, real insight (in my opinion). But to tell you the truth, I can't be sure I answered anything because I'm being translated. Here's how it went: When I said a lot, I'd pause, so the translator could translate. To that my translator would respond, "Go on." So I did. But then, when I'd say a little bit, he'd translate for a really long time, and we continued with that back and forth, standing next to each other on stage.

After my session, I had no idea if I connected with the audience through the translation. Things get lost. The rest of the speakers present, the same translator translates. We do interviews, he translates. After a full eight-hour day of presentations, the conference is over. So we're all relaxing at the mixer and the three international presenters and I are acknowledging the translator's work. We're all realizing that this dude was working harder than any of us individually because he translated the whole day—four presentations and four panel discussions.

As I was thanking the translator along with the group, he turned to me and said, "Actually, I've never translated before and I didn't know how to communicate most of what you guys were saying." After a deafening silence, brief pause, and deep eye gaze to confirm that he wasn't joking I replied, "This was worth it for the story."

The takeaway here is that you, your firm, and the client can only get by for so long sitting in the meeting nodding your heads when you actually don't understand each other. The gulf between understanding each other could be as wide as the Grand Canyon or as simple as semantics (for example, B-school professor Kevin Keller's "Points of Parity and Points of Differentiation" concept equals D-school "Compare and Contrast" concept). Either way, it distracts our focus from the communication barrier between the brand and the target. It also creates a communication barrier between members of the same team. The bottom line: If you're not fluent in the language spoken in the room, then you can't communicate.

Same Book, Different Translation

At some point you'll find yourself trying to communicate to an audience or a team who knows exactly what you are saying, but has no idea what you mean. Think of it like this: In England a pram is what we call a stroller in America. Two people might be talking about the same product or project but have no idea that's the case. Semantics. In our field, art directors in advertising agencies have a very different job than art directors in design firms. At an agency, an art director works with a copywriting partner to conceptualize and design the work. In a design firm, the same job title may have designers reporting to him or her in more of a supervisory role.

Context. If you've never worked in one or the other, it would be very confusing when you show up for your new gig and try to figure out the pecking order.

Whether communication snafus arise because of a terminology jargon issue, or because the members of your team aren't all exposed to certain concepts, lack of understanding is a problem. The first step to moving beyond that problem is determining the root of it. Should your group define some terms? Should there be more clarity on roles or diversity of effort on the team? From there, you can devise a strategy to align everyone on the client goals.

Perspectives on "Success"

Believe it or not, the team might not even be on the same page when it comes to defining success. As designers, art directors, writers, or creatives, our point of view about what works or what doesn't work can seem completely opposite from what "the suits"—account management, new-business team, marketing folks, or clients—think. This is because:

▸ Creatives are focused on creativity and how beautiful or unique the work can be.

▸ Account management is focused on pleasing the client.

▸ The new-business team is focused on winning new accounts.

▸ The marketers are focused on moving the needle in a way that they can prove with metrics.

We all begin with our own unique point of view, but this isn't the root problem. All of these goals are important. The real issue is the difficulty in understanding that regardless of what side of the brain you think with, we are all trying to achieve the same result, what I call *creative business solutions*.

Noticing these varying goals is the easy part. Truly understanding each other's viewpoint is not. Understanding takes energy. Understanding demands active listening skills. Understanding requires translation. Understanding needs a new vocabulary. When you truly understand where everyone else is coming from, you can achieve perspective about how your part factors into the whole. I only know this from a career's worth of making mistakes that have reinforced the fact that it's not easy to understand the whole. I wanted to argue from *my* point of view. "They" didn't understand and "they" were stupid on top of that. How could "they" not see that this was the exact typeface we should be using? It was completely clear to me that these colors made the composition beautiful. "They" must be blind. Why couldn't "they" see the most obvious things? "They" just didn't get it and it made me mad.

It took time for me to see things from *their* perspective. To a marketer, that font seemed off brand or off target, and therefore off strategy. To the account manager, that font seemed inconsistent with the client's conservative brand guidelines. To the new-business team,

the font wasn't large enough to provide the impact we were going for to win the business. So depending on whose perspective we are looking at, *we* are "they."

So what do we do? We understand the other perspectives by learning the objectives behind clients' requests and shift our focus to that. That provides the clarity by shifting these decisions away from an individual's preference and toward connecting the brand with the target.

If You Had to Explain It to Your Mother

Tibor Kalman, "the bad boy" of graphic design, is often quoted as saying, "We are here to inject art into commerce." It took me some time to realize this, but the truth is that advertising and design exist to achieve a business or marketing objective. What we are doing stems from the business or marketing objectives that everyone must reach, and how we should do it designwise is the way we get there. If you began your career (like I did) as a pure creative, then you were probably called in after the conversation discussing the business and marketing objectives. Now, it's time to get the designer. As a result, much or all of what I'll mention ahead will be familiar to you because you will have designed some or all of it. Yet you (justifiably) might not have a good understanding of the points behind what you were asked to design. I sure didn't.

When working now, I focus my visual, verbal, and conceptual thinking on design options that achieve the business and marketing objectives. The work should be beautiful—and effective at achieving the awareness objectives, spiking new member acquisition, driving traffic, or building the company e-mail list. Thinking this way will help you focus on design options that are viable and creative and that increase the probability that you will be on strategy.

Depending upon your organization's process, these objectives may be worked out ahead of time without the creative team. Other times, the client will request a tactical deliverable (such as a website) when they really need strategic solutions that accomplish specific objectives (such as an increase in digital sales). Either way, there is a range of business or marketing objectives, and understanding them in detail will allow you to lead your client in whatever role you find yourself in. As you read these, think of practical ways that you can apply these concepts to problems you are solving at work or for your freelance clients.

ESTABLISHING OR CHANGING PERCEPTIONS

Let's say that you are working on a new product launch (the Apple watch), refreshing an old product/service (a new and improved Motel 6), or repositioning a product or service that has lost its customers' trust (such as Volkswagen, Chobani, or Naked Juice).

The marketing objectives for dealing with customers' perceptions would most likely include:

1. Making the target customers aware of this new product

2. Communicating product or service benefits in the language and style the target would be receptive to

3. Positioning the product relative to its competitors in the target's mind

4. Establishing a brand preference among the potential choices

5. Re-establishing positive brand attributes and values

6. Loyalty or increased frequency of purchase

7. Increasing social media engagement around a brand, product, or service

SUPPORTING PURCHASE

Many products and services are complex and need additional parts or care beyond the initial purchase, such as a car. The company would want to inform customers of service plans, support websites, call centers, or service locations. The brand would most likely want to welcome new customers in a series of communications aimed at educating them about all that the new service has to offer.

The business objectives for supporting a purchase would most likely include:

1. Acquiring customers into an insurance, installation, or maintenance plan online or by direct mail

2. Decreasing the cost of live phone customer service by driving customers online (websites or social media) to troubleshoot themselves

3. Driving customers online to schedule appointments or pickups

4. Retaining a high level of customer/brand engagement through e-mail content with deep links to the website

5. Cross-selling related products or upselling additional services based on purchase behavior

EDUCATION

As new products (smartphones, tablets, wearables, etc.) are developed and technology advances, companies introduce new communication platforms (think Facebook, WhatsApp, Snapchat, Tumblr, Pinterest, etc.) to ensure that people understand how these products could benefit them (for example, campaigns developed to explain how smartwatches could be leveraged in everyday life). The education objective is crucial to helping consumers understand the differences in similar products when they comparison shop as well.

The marketing objectives to educate consumers would most likely include:

1. Specifying minimum compatibility requirements

2. Demonstrating the product's features and ease of use

3. Driving prospects to a website to learn more or capturing e-mail addresses for newsletters

4. Increasing frequency of use and expanding user activities with the new product

5. Increasing app downloads

6. Highlighting a product's benefits or differences relative to the competition

FOSTERING AND PROMOTING BRAND ADVOCACY

After you've purchased a new Dyson Ball vacuum cleaner and you watch the commercials or see the billboards, you feel a part of that group. This reinforces your decision to purchase that product. It could also make you more likely to remember that brand in a favorable way and buy additional products from the same company.

The marketing objectives to promote brand advocacy would most likely include:

1. Increasing sharing from a customer to his or her friends

2. Increasing favorable product reviews on websites

3. Increasing word-of-mouth referral visits to retailers

DRIVING SALES

Increasing sales is the overall objective of any initiative, but here I'll focus on things that immediately move the needle in a short period of time. These include promotions, coupons, sweepstakes that need point-of-purchase displays, counter cards, risers, advertorials. For example, think of the decreasing cost and increasing size of Ultra HD 4K LED TVs, seasonal McRib sandwiches at McDonalds, and back-to-school or year-end car sales.

The business or marketing objectives for driving sales would most likely include:

1. Building a list of prospects based on the best current customers

2. Increasing overall purchase amounts

3. Liquidating a certain product to make room for another

Do Unto Others As Marketers Do Unto You

While looking over this list of common business objectives, you may have begun to visualize the type of communication needed based on the objective. If so, this illustrates the fact that it's easier for creatives to arrive at a relevant strategic communication when they clearly understand the objective.

It's always a good exercise to see how these communications have shown up in your own life. Look in your Inbox and mailbox at home to recognize these business and marketing objectives in the offers that have targeted you.

Step 1: Find any ad or promotion in any channel. Grab a magazine, open your promotions tab in Gmail, or find a video/TV spot. Any marketing message will do.

Step 2: Identify the objective(s) of the marketing material. There is a reason for this piece—likely one of the business or marketing objectives just listed. Can you find it?

Step 3: Identify the message of the marketing material. What do they want the target, reader, or viewer to take away from the material? Looking at the language used and visual elements, briefly sum up what they are trying to communicate about the brand, product, or service.

Step 4: Identify what the call to action is. Now that the target has read and received the message, what steps is he or she instructed to take to receive the benefit?

When I understood these objectives, I began to see that this was less about what I liked about the typeface and more about what was most persuasive to the target, as a means to achieve the business objective. Being on brand, on strategy, and on message with every element of the work is what makes it viable.

What "They" Say versus What "They" Need

Though our clients, whether internal or external, come to us for a variety of very different reasons, projects, budgets, and scopes of work, they basically show up with different forms of the exact same request: "Solve my problem." They, like any other person needing an expert, arrive in front of you wanting your professional opinion of the viable options they have—that is, they want your leadership. Knowing this, we can read between the lines to identify what they *really* need and fight the impulse to simply respond tactically. We need to determine the business and marketing objectives that should guide the way forward.

"Solve my problem" is not how the request is communicated to us. The request usually sounds like "I need a website," "We need a new logo," or "It's time to update our packaging." But none of these requests really hit at the heart of what the client's business or marketing objectives are. That's where your work as a translator comes in.

THEY SAY: I need a website.

WE HEAR: They need a cool website! (a tactical request)

Most of us who went to D-school were taught to focus on the tactical parts of strategic decisions: the finished product, the details, what it looks like, the colors, the typefaces,

the layout. But if you respond to a tactical request with only a tactical outcome, you are leaving strategy out of the equation and miss the bigger picture of what our creative business solutions are supposed to achieve. Yet the bigger picture is exactly why we are all in the room, to find the strategic approach with the most effective design execution. In order to get more perspective, I'm proposing that we dig a little deeper and learn to hear the request a bit differently.

Let's face it: If you get vague direction from the client ("I need a website"), it's because they don't know exactly how to communicate their objectives. They're looking to you as the expert.

I believe this is the opportunity we miss to make the client's relationship with us much more valuable than the "just get it done" transactional relationships we've all had. Sure, they need a new website. Now that that's established, isolate the key business objective—i.e., what the organization needs the website to accomplish. This will be how they will define success. And they'll need to hit certain goals within that definition to move the needle on the way to achieving that success. If we can focus the creative team while developing our recommendations with that definition in mind, I can assure you that you'll have their attention when proposing solutions. Now you're focused on solving their strategic job responsibilities through design.

THEY SAY: I need a website.

WHAT WE CAN TRANSLATE:
The Marketing Objectives
(wrapped in a cool website)

Knowing what they're trying to accomplish with the website lets us translate their wishes into realizable design objectives. They might want to:

▸ Increase traffic

▸ Increase repeat and unique visits

▸ Increase number of page views, increase time on site

▸ Increase average order value

▸ Increase pass-along value

▸ Facilitate brand advocacy

For example, the head of e-commerce will need to increase digital sales, therefore the website she asked for will need to be responsive, should be optimized for SEM (search engine marketing) and SEO (search engine optimization), and will need a component to drive traffic and extend its reach through being easily shareable in social media.

When you dig deeper, you see that her actual needs are a lot more complicated than the original request.

THEY SAY: We need a new logo.

WHAT WE CAN TRANSLATE:
The Business Objectives

A request for a logo usually has a lot of business objectives behind it. For example, a brand manager is responsible for the product portfolio strategy. Therefore, that logo he requested will need to be part of a larger identity or packaging that should facilitate loyalty and be distinctive enough to remain top-of-mind when the consumer is considering a purchase in that category.

YOUR ROLE AS TRANSLATOR WILL OPEN DOORS
These types of translations are how you unlock the difference between a one-time transaction and a long-term relationship with your client. Get to the root of why they need what they're requesting. Once you've gotten their attention with your strategic approach, they're more likely to be willing to take creative risks with you. Speak to the business objectives that keep the client up at night and see what happens. You'll probably have a similar experience as I did: Once, after being awarded a sizable account, I asked my new client, "Why'd you choose my team?" The client responded, "Because you challenged us." This was my confirmation that I addressed the key business objectives and understood what the people who were responsible for the business needed to accomplish. Get to the reason behind the request.

Turning Words Into Inspiration

Getting to the root of exactly what the client wants sounds like it should be easy, but it often isn't. Yet everyone needs to agree on and understand the goals of the campaign before you go any further into the process. That's why it's so important to broaden your creative horizons to better grasp business goals.

- Everyone on the team—from creatives to the suits—has a different measure of success. Aligning those with specific business and marketing objectives helps everyone get on the same page.

- Sometimes the client or suits won't ask you for exactly what they need. Read between the lines to find actual business objectives behind their tactical requests. This is what they really need.

- Strategic approaches to creative solutions are grounded in facts and better suited to build long-lasting campaigns on.

PART II

Finding Inspiration in Order: Gathering and Organizing Information

4 You Talkin' to Me?

Reaching Your Target on Behalf of the Brand

I'll never forget the day I noticed something disturbing about the way Burger King communicated to me while watching music videos on Black Entertainment Television. Visually, the commercial was simply the letters "BK4U" in distressed "urban" typography as if graffiti-ed on a brick wall. While on the screen, what sounded like an African-American male voice chanted "B-K-4-U" several times over video of a mouthwatering flame-broiled Whopper being assembled. I'm sure there were any number of descriptive adjectives specific to why the Whopper was the burger for me. The truth is, it would have worked except for one thing: I specifically remember thinking to myself at 22, "Why did they choose to talk to me that way? I don't speak that way."

The commercial was on the right channel to reach a young African-American male, interested in hip hop music and a frequent Burger King customer. The effectiveness of the commercial is obvious, because I can still recall it today (for the wrong reasons). However, the broken communication spoken "at" me assumed a homogeneous target, a stereotype even. I was familiar with the rap-like delivery of the voice-over and the "urban" graphic type-style, but in the end I felt patronized. At the time, I had no knowledge of advertising, marketing, demographics, or psychographics. I just knew that on other television channels, I "saw" a concept and "heard" Burger King speak in plain English using complete sentences.

Speak Like a Native

Your design, packaging, or creative concept should be so on target that women responding to your website for birth control should have no idea if it was designed by a man. The upscale audience for the Maserati you are designing for should have no idea that you aren't rich. Work for any ethnic groups should strike the right tone so as to not hinder communication.

My experience with the Burger King commercial serves as my reminder to seek to understand the diverse groups I speak to on behalf of clients. And it's bigger than just color. The psychographic nuances (or attitudes and beliefs of subsegments within a specific group or surrounding a certain product) span across cultures. This fact serves as the basis to increase representation of all voices in advertising and design—not just the underrepresented ones. Getting the details and tone right not only facilitates communication with every potential customer, it actually increases the probability of being heard. The key is to first understand that you are not the target and then to fully immerse yourself in learning who the target is.

The bottom line is that all voices are needed, both in front of and behind the concept, marketing plan, or digital strategy. This defines the role of an advertising or design practitioner and will be what defines success in an ever-changing dialogue. The successful student or professional will be skilled in creating an ongoing dialogue around

products and services. To cultivate one-to-one relationships, brands will need professionals who have been trained to integrate a relevant message into a variety of channels.

Now that you are familiar with

▸ the words behind the pictures—key business terms you need to know,

▸ being unified with the team crafting messages,

▸ features, benefits, and values, and

▸ the creative strategy framework,

we can move forward to obtain a greater understanding of the connections between the brand and the target. In this chapter, we will delve into getting to know and understand the target's wants and needs enough to align the right elements within a strategy to inspire relevant work.

Getting Through the Clutter

We are all bombarded with thousands of marketing messages or ads a day. In order for your message to cut through the clutter, it must not only look beautiful, it has to be relevant. Yet even "beautiful and relevant" is not enough. The message must also be delivered in a channel that the target is most likely to come in contact with. Have you ever wondered when you were being briefed on a project, *Why are we designing this as a print newspaper ad again? Does our target still read those?* Or *It's cool we are designing this app, but wouldn't the text be too small for senior citizens?* Maybe you've wondered in the back of your mind if the teens you were developing the website for were most likely to access the Internet through their phones or communicate through social media exclusively.

Other times, the question concerns the credibility of the tone or format of the communications. Is that how this brand usually communicates visually? Sometimes things just don't add up. Your instincts as a designer may alert you when something is off and the approach, channel, or design doesn't seem within the brand's personality. These types of decisions on where and how to build the relationship between the brand and the target are important decisions the client is concerned with— and they may be looking to you for a recommendation.

Many a marketing team and brand manager are concerned with:

▸ Increasing repeat sales through engaging the target customer

▸ Developing communications that are in line with the brand and differentiate the product or service they are trying to sell

▸ Integrating the brand in a unified way across multiple touchpoints or channels

Over time, I've come to understand that relevance equals response. Whether you are tasked with developing the identity for a brand's launch or are part of a team tasked with defining or redefining its core values, a deep understanding of the brand and target is essential. Let's start with the brand.

Whom Are We Speaking For? Seeking Inspiration Within the Brand/Product/Service

Reaching your target is a lot easier when you know the brand well. What is a "brand"? The American Marketing Association (AMA) defines a brand as "a name, term, design, symbol, or any other feature that identifies one seller's good or service as distinct from those of other sellers." Brand legend and American Institute of Graphic Arts (AIGA) medalist Walter Landor puts it this way on the AIGA website: "Products are made in the factory, but brands are created in the mind."

In the *Harvard Business Review* "Case Study: Brands and Branding," author Douglas B. Holt defines a brand in personal terms as "the product as experienced and valued by the customer in everyday life."

However you best understand what a brand is, these quotes help clarify the marketing and business objectives you're likely to encounter. You may have heard terms like *brand differentiation*, *brand preference*, and *brand loyalty*. These are some of the most sought-after goals. Understanding what's in a brand's heritage will help you and your team tell stories using the tangible aspects of the brand most familiar to creatives. (Search YouTube for "Johnnie Walker: The Man Who Walked Around the World" for a brilliant example of using brand heritage in storytelling.)

TAPPING INTO A BRAND'S VALUES

I love this quote from publisher and author William Feather: "The philosophy behind much advertising is based on the old observation that every man is really two men—the man he is and the man he wants to be." When you look closely, you can see that companies do indeed play to both consumers. Companies post their manifestos in stores, "go green," and go to great lengths to tell the public what their values are. Be sure you are taking your client's values into account when you think of creative solutions.

You can break down the brand into a few components:

- The **identity** of the brand is expressed in its logo, typography, color palette, packaging, and retail environment.

- The **tone** of the brand is expressed in the attitude of the copy, voice-over, or composition of the layout.

- The **values** of the brand are expressed in the channels the brand's messaging is communicated in, the associations or partnerships it fosters, and the processes the brand uses to do business (think recycling for environmental values, or charities the brand donates to for social or cultural values).

Know Thy Target Like the Back of Thy Hand

Now for the target. When they need to be reminded, I'll ask my creative teams, "Why do jeans have two legs?" Sensing that this may be a trick question but unsure why I'm asking something I clearly know the answer to, they respond with the obvious answer. The point is my version of the modern architectural and industrial design principle "form follows function." The reason you design a print campaign should be that your target reads periodicals in paper format. The reason you create an app should be the quantifiable fact that your target makes up a significant portion of smartphone users.

It all starts from an intimate knowledge of your target. Their media behavior, or how they access information, should determine where you communicate to them. With this understanding, it's important that you research or are given a clear picture of whom you are talking to. This may seem obvious, but I am often surprised at how vague descriptions of the ideal customer for a product or service can be. If you aren't given exact specifics in the form of demographics, psychographics, and behavioral and attitudinal characteristics, you are basically stabbing in the dark. Seek clarity from the appropriate people when your target isn't clear. Doing this will save you and the creative team countless hours of execution time. Do it right or do it twice.

The Reasons Behind the Purchase

As you get to know your target through studying their behavior, now you can seek to understand the values and psychology behind why they do what they do.

Most marketing and business programs mention Maslow's hierarchy of needs when delving into consumer behavior. Saul McLeod of SimplyPsychology.org explains it this way: "Maslow wanted to understand what motivates people. He believed that people possess a set of motivation systems unrelated to rewards or unconscious desires. Maslow (1943) stated that people are motivated to achieve certain needs. When one need is fulfilled a person seeks to fulfill the next one, and so on."

MASLOW'S HIERARCHY OF NEEDS

Self-actualization
Morality, creativity, spontaneity, problem solving, lack of prejudice, acceptance of facts

Esteem
Self-esteem, confidence, achievement, respect of others

Love/Belonging
Friendship, family, sexual intimacy

Safety
Security of body, of employment, of resources, of morality, of family, of health, of property

Physiological
Breathing, food, water, sex, sleep, homeostasis, excretion

SO MASLOW AND I WALKED INTO A BAR

It also wouldn't hurt to mention the Maslovian approach in your pitch, justification, or strategy if it helped you arrive at an insight. This could even raise trust (and eyebrows) among the suits when they hear that your creative solutions are rooted in principles of psychology. For example, when talking about the underlying need that the target has for esteem or status based on their lifestyle choices and purchase history, we would justify a crest design element, gold foil on the packaging, or the strategy to position the product as higher quality because of the price. It's our job to understand and then leverage underlying motivations within the target to build a connection with the brand.

If you look at the diagram, you'll see that at the most basic level are the needs that sustain life itself, or biological and physiological needs. At the top is the more abstract need of self-actualization. When brainstorming creative approaches or developing potential solutions, try to understand the underlying motivation the target has for the product. This approach may inspire some interesting questions. For example, think of the "Reassuringly Expensive" tagline used by the Belgian lager Stella Artois from 1982 to 2007 in the UK. Though this was the creative business solution to turn a negative (higher prices due to import duties) into a positive, it makes the point that there is something deeper driving the outward behavior.

Brand Preference

Most of us have become weary of marketing messaging and therefore most of us avoid them when we can and ignore them when we can't. However, there are some brands that probably have your undivided attention. So what's the difference? In order to figure out why certain brands "speak" to you, identify your favorite brand in a category or two—your favorite ice cream, ski resort, or car company. The reasons could be based on what is actual (what you do now) or aspirational (how you'd like to be perceived)—it doesn't matter because they are your favorites for a reason and it's time to understand why. Ask yourself these questions:

- What is it about the language that is used in the ads, brochure, video, packaging, or website that speaks to you? Why?

- What words do they use that catch your attention and what do they mean to you?

- What underlying Maslow need are they speaking to in you?

When you can articulate these answers for yourself, you'll be better equipped to choose the right vocabulary for your targets.

- Maslow's hierarchy of needs can help you pinpoint the underlying reason driving the purchase of a product or service. Zero in on what the real need is that is being addressed so your creative solutions speak directly to it.

- Identify why your favorite brands capture your loyalty. Personalizing the experience gives you an intimate knowledge of how to understand the target's choices.

Turning Words Into Inspiration

Once you learn to speak the language like a native, and can determine the underlying need for what your client is selling, you can use visual language to speak in a way that prospects want to hear. Remember these points:

- Your target should not see the designers or team behind the work, only the brand in front of them. Your language and visuals should connect the brand and the target through consistency.

- To get to know your target on a deeper level, let them tell you who they are through their behavior. The more familiar you are with a target, the more effectively you can speak to them.

5 The Cord-Cutter Struggle

Understanding Features, Benefits, and Values

Recently I purchased the two Sony UHD TVs I'd been researching in Best Buy for some time, and as a result needed to think through our streaming solutions. Over the years I had been watching the larger TVs become less and less expensive, even as the quality of the overall picture improved. As cord-cutters, our viewing behavior centers around streaming *House of Cards* on Netflix and *Dancing with the Stars* on Hulu, ordering movies like *Star Wars* on Vudu, and so on. As you know, the benefit of not subscribing to cable means you watch whatever you want, as much as you want, when you want, without expensive bundles or a show forcing you on the couch when it's on. Those of you who also view your media without cable know that, when you upgrade your TV platforms, the effort and research to connect all the dots in a new ecosystem begins anew.

So I found myself in the market for a new streaming solution for that one big hole in my new setup. After reading numerous reviews and watching product reviews on Apple TV, Amazon Fire TV, TiVo, and Roku, it was time to Uber on over to Best Buy.

As I made my way to the electronics section, I had my eye on three main products: Roku Streaming Stick, Amazon Fire TV Stick, and Apple TV. As I read each product's packaging, I'd be joined by two women in their late fifties (one even had an Apple watch) all considering the same things that I was: online reviews, our personal preferences and needs, features, price, availability, compatibility, ease of user interface, and so on. After carefully considering each feature and the benefit it would provide for me in the context of my wants and needs, I'm happy with the results of my decision—or would be if only I could get faster Internet speeds.

Value to the Consumer Is Expressed As Features and Benefits

In Chapter 3, we covered the business and marketing objectives that brands are out to achieve, and my adventure in Best Buy highlights the importance of clearly articulated features and benefits during the education phase of the consumer journey. These items are what allow consumers to understand and weigh the points of parity (how these products are the same) with the points of differentiation (how these products are different) to arrive at the right decision for them. My companions in the electronics aisle at Best Buy—the two tech-savvy grandmothers—were looking at the same set of products I was, and though we came to different conclusions based on the features and benefits, we all needed to educate ourselves before making our decisions. Our underlying values were similar: We could no longer see the point of wasting hundreds of dollars on hundreds of bundled channels we didn't watch.

In this chapter, we'll explore in depth the features, benefits, and values that enable brands to differentiate themselves.

As a creative, you'll want to focus on what the consumer should take away from your design, advertising, website, or event—and in a nutshell, that is the value of the product or service to the consumer. Brand strategist and author David Aaker frames this concept in his book *Strategic Market Management*: "Ultimately the offering needs to appeal to new and existing customers. There needs to be a value proposition that is relevant and meaningful to the customer and is reflected in the positioning of the product or service. To support a successful strategy, it should be sustainable over time and be differentiated from competitors."

For creatives, the relevant part to take away from this is that the client, account, marketing, and business departments are looking for visual and verbal messaging to differentiate the product from its competitors. It's obvious that we comparison shop and look for the best value for the money. As a result, your work must present the features (the physical attributes of a brand, product, or service) and the specific benefits (what it does for the target consumer). When this is done well, it becomes easier for a potential customer to determine how one digital camera may be a better choice for landscapes than another, or why a particular running shoe may be a better fit for her, based on her need for balance or support.

Strategic positioning or differentiation isn't possible without presenting the target with the most compelling information about the features and benefits. *When we as creatives can look at this through the lens of finding the common values that exist between the brand and the target, the result is a more profitable relationship with satisfied customers.* This was one of the most important lessons I learned over the course of my time at NYU. The gentleman I learned it from was professor Neil Feinstein. Neil is an expert on building brands and relationships with the customers they serve. I first met Neil after landing a freelance gig at the agency where he was a longtime creative strategist. I then took one of his classes, where he taught me the fundamentals of inspiring creatives through a good brief. Over time, we would become freelance creative partners on several brands and eventually colleagues during my time on the faculty at NYU. I've learned a great deal from Neil and it is my pleasure to introduce him as the first of five professional partners I've invited to collaborate with me on this book. So without further ado, Neil Feinstein, Assistant Professor of Mass Communication, now at St. John's University.

▶ Features versus Benefits
by Neil Feinstein

I have a lot of experience in the financial sector, having developed multiple strategies and programs for blue chip companies such as American Express, Chase, Prudential, and Merrill Lynch. Finance is a highly regulated industry and corporate lawyers take particular care to ensure that advertising copy does not make irresponsible claims or promises. I can't tell you how many times my copy was redlined because I was demonstrating how, for example, a low credit card interest rate could make that big-screen TV you always wanted more accessible.

The lawyers' job was to protect the bank against being sued. My job was to make the product seem as desirable as possible so consumers would want it. (Considering that credit cards are not all that sexy, this is a formidable task.) Please know this was not adversarial, but always involved a negotiation. In a highly regulated category like finance, attorneys and creatives always collaborate to find ways to make the product desirable without putting a company at risk.

The conflict typically hinged around the benefit. The promise. The thing that would make a consumer desire the product. From an attorney's point of view, it's prudent to word things conservatively. From a marketer's perspective, it's a mistake. To know why, it's critical to understand the role features and benefits play in motivating a sale. Here's how you tell the difference.

FEATURE, DEFINED

Features (also called attributes) are key characteristics of the product or service: Air bags in a car. Extra legroom in your seat on a plane. Tacos on the menu. Over the years I've found the best way to identify features is to answer this question:

What does the product offer?

BENEFIT, DEFINED

As marketers, we are in the business of creating customers, which is why we should look at selling from the customer's point of view. So we always ladder product features up to benefits, because benefits focus on the consumer's needs or desires. That's what precipitates a sale.

A benefit is the advantage a consumer gets from a product. Another way to look at it is that benefits answer this question:

What's in it for me?

WHY STRESS BENEFITS OVER FEATURES?

At the core of every advertising message is its ability to make a product or service relevant to the consumer. Features don't do that. Benefits do. So the primary job of a creative is to translate a feature into a meaningful benefit that will motivate a sale and begin a relationship.

The process starts with a deep knowledge of the consumer. What does s/he care about? How does the product fit into his/her life? The answers to these questions lead you to the product benefits, which should be the foundation for *all* creative decisions: the written words, the chosen pictures, the hired actors, even the animations that are built.

Here's a way to prove you understand the difference. Below are features of well-known products. Translate each feature into a benefit that's important to the identified audience. For example, the feature of extra legroom turns into the benefit of a more comfortable ride. The airbag features translate into a safety benefit.

Product	Target Audience	Feature (What does the product offer?)	Benefit (What's in it for me?)
Planet Fitness	People who want to get in shape without feeling like a loser	No "lunkheads" allowed	You won't feel intimidated every time you work out.
The Disney Rewards VISA Card	Moms	Comes with 0% vacation financing	Save money on your trip.
Nike running shoes	Weekend athletes	Built-in extra cushioning	Your knees won't hurt when you go running.

According the Philip Kotler and Hermawan Kartajaya in *Future Model for Marketing 3.0* (the age of collaboration), "in Marketing 3.0, marketers should target consumers' minds and spirits simultaneously to touch their hearts. Positioning will trigger the mind to consider a buying decision. . . . [D]ifferentiation [will] confirm the decision. . . . [T]he heart will lead a consumer to act and make the buying decision." Based on Kotler and Kartajaya, the primary driver of a purchase is the heart. The emotions. But benefits tend to be rational: 0% financing means you'll save money. Is that enough to compel a consumer to open an account? Probably not. So how can a creative trigger emotions? With values.

Values, at their core, are emotional. And emotions activate behavior.

Values have worth. Values go far beyond usefulness to have emotional meaning. They are different for every person, so values are personal. Values answer the question:

Why should I care?

When you build a case for your product with a consumer and incorporate values, you give a compelling reason why your product is critical in his or her life.

Let's practice. Layer in the values to the previous exercise.

Product	Target Audience	Feature (What does the product offer?)	Benefit (What's in it for me?)	Value (Why should I care?)
Planet Fitness	People who want to get in shape without feeling like a loser	No "lunkheads" allowed	You won't feel intimidated every time you work out.	Feel confident as you get healthier.
The Disney Rewards VISA Card	Moms	Comes with 0% vacation financing	Save money on your trip.	A magical family experience at an affordable price.
Nike running shoes	Weekend athletes	Built-in extra cushioning	Your knees won't hurt when you go running.	Look great. Feel great.

A Classic Example of a Brand's Features, Benefits, and Values

Let's consider the features, benefits, and values of Mountain Dew. This carbonated soft drink is loaded with caffeine (the **feature**). The target is young men with a zest for life. The benefit of caffeine is that it gives you energy. But simply "giving you energy" is not specific enough to create a value, because it can mean something different to everyone: Dunkin' Donuts has built their brand on the energy that keeps you going throughout your busy day.

How did Mountain Dew ladder the energy benefit to a value that was meaningful to their young, energetic male audience? They turned energy into extreme exhilaration. That's what young men care about. If you look at their advertising, it shows young men playing extreme sports with pounding music in the background. They embody exhilaration and make Mountain Dew the drink that makes life more fun, which is the ultimate value.

By turning caffeine into exhilaration, Mountain Dew connects with their audience and gives them a compelling reason to choose Mountain Dew over any other soft drink. This strategy is proven time and again to build brand preference and drive purchase behavior.

That's why features are fine, but benefits are better. And values rule. ∎

11 COPYWRITING TIPS by Neil Feinstein

As you consider the features, benefits, and values of whatever you're working on now, try to employ these tips as you craft your positioning copy.

1. Read what you wrote aloud.

2. Pay attention to the rhythm. Vary sentence length.

3. Don't tell them what they already know. Tell them something new.

4. Always answer the question "Why should I care?"

5. Focus on benefits.

6. Imply urgency.

7. Touch the reader's heart and mind.

8. Tell them what you want them to do.

9. Don't tell me how to feel. Make me feel.

10. Write like a person, not a professor.

11. Edit. Edit. Edit.

If Your Offer Isn't Relevant, It Is Meaningless

After Neil's explanation, I hope you have a deeper understanding of features and benefits. You'll need it to find creative solutions that are truly rooted in the target's common values with the brand. The words "relevant" and "meaningful" in David Aaker's quote at the beginning of this chapter remind me of the conversation with my cable company retention specialist when I called to cancel cable in the first place.

Me: Hi, I'm calling to cancel cable and phone service. I just want the Internet.

Cable guy: You'll lose your discount on all the services if you cancel cable and phone—the Internet service will cost more by itself.

Me: We don't even own a home phone so it doesn't make sense to pay for something each month that we don't even use, and the only channels we watch are Discovery and History Channels. We read our news and stream everything else on Netflix, Hulu, and Amazon.

Cable guy: What if we bring your bill down 30 dollars, would you keep the Internet, cable, and phone bundle?

Me: We don't even own a home phone, and we only watch two channels.

Cable guy: I can throw in premium movie channels Showtime, Starz, and Encore for a year, so you can keep Discovery and History Channels with the bundle. If you're like me, I watch that show *Power* on Starz and with the bundle, you can watch football and basketball on ESPN and boxing on Showtime.

Me: I don't want to pay for a home phone, and I don't really watch *Power*, football, or basketball, we only watch two channels and that isn't worth paying for cable.

Cable guy: I see what you mean.

As this conversation demonstrates, the features and benefits in the value proposition were not relevant to me anymore, even for free. At the root of this, I value paying only for what I'm using, so as not to waste money. There was nothing short of a two-channel, a-la-carte Discovery and History Channels–only bundle (which they don't have) with no phone that could keep me.

This conversation further reminds me as a creative to make sure that I'm:

▸ Choosing relevant features.

▸ Finding benefits that align with the attitudes, behaviors, and values of the target I'm trying to reach.

Remember to ask yourself: "Does the target care about that?" when choosing the features and benefits in your proposition.

Turning Words Into Inspiration

Here are a few tips to keep in mind when breaking down a brand, product, or service into features/benefits/values. First, remember these definitions:

Features = What a brand or product offers?

Benefits = What it does for me, the target? Values = Why should I, the target, care?

The features of a product or service are similar to the physical features of a person. Think about your phone: touch screen, front-facing camera, storage capacity, and network are all features. These features enable specific benefits such as ease of use, a visual and verbal connection, and freedom to star in your own creativity, accumulate memories, and change your theme song on the fly. A target group's values will be determined by what is important to that group. Oftentimes these values are used to make decisions and this is where there is room for common ground with a brand.

▸ In general, it is best to list one feature with a corresponding benefit so that you can pinpoint what benefit comes from what feature.

▸ If you work with a writer, happen to be a writer, or are responsible for presentations in your job, you'll need to hone your writing skills. Another pair of eyes can't hurt—always ask for someone to check over your work. You should always evaluate each aspect of your presentation—even the parts you aren't responsible for. Anyone can catch a mistake or make a suggestion that may lead to a better end product.

▸ It is important to make an exhaustive list of each of these features and identify the corresponding benefits the features provide to the consumer. From this, your team will uncover how the product or service is unique from its competitors. As a result, creative exploration can accentuate or focus on presenting these differentiating characteristics and the benefits in the different directions.

▸ When taking the elements from your features and benefits list and turning them into the creative product, decide if your audience would be more susceptible to a feature statement or a benefit statement in the creative approach. Consider the product, service or brand's heritage, competitors, business category, and channel that your message is being communicated in. Also think through the customer's journey or decision-making process.

▸ Use your list of features and benefits to write a variety of concepts based on common values.

▸ Use feature- and benefit-inspired headlines to achieve the objective or articulate the message.

▸ Organize and match these features and benefits with a relevant target to accomplish client objectives with the creative strategy framework in Chapter 6.

6 Think How They Think to Do What We Do

Implementing the Creative Strategy Framework

Chances are that you've heard the quote "the whole is *greater* than the sum of its parts" but that's actually not what the Gestalt psychologist Kurt Koffka said. When this was translated into English from German, it turns out that the word "greater" was substituted for his original word choice, "other." According to Dr. Russ Dewey's textbook *Psychology: An Introduction,*

"Koffka did not like that translation. He firmly corrected students who substituted 'greater' for 'other' (Heider, 1977). 'This is not a principle of addition,' he said. The statement as originally worded was supposed to mean that the whole had an *independent existence* in the perceptual system.

"[T]he whole is 'other' than the sum of its parts."

It seems to me that Koffka's observations were the clearest explanation for the magic that happens in the creative process when all the individual elements are leveraged correctly. Something *other* happens. I guess you could argue that the butterfly is *greater* than the caterpillar, but it seems to me that argument would miss the magic of the caterpillar turning into the butterfly. At its best, what is inspired by the strategic entertains, educates, and resonates with its target on a deeper level than just buying and selling. The work we create, whether visual or verbal, is magic inspired by the sum of its parts. To harness that inspiration, this chapter will focus on the organization and quality of those parts.

Finding Order in Chaos: Context

Designers work in various levels of order and chaos. And yes, a large percentage of that chaos is internal. It seems to come with the gift of creativity. However, the external chaos is a combination of the do-it-now culture we work in and the people we work with. A creative project kickoff can range anywhere from a very organized formal briefing to a haphazard, vague Word document attached to an e-mail. I've often left briefing meetings with either too much or irrelevant information—but have never left with *all* the information. And even then, *all* the information must be whittled down to the *right* information. Yet the expectation on us all is basically the same: Make it pretty by the deadline.

The best part of this is that even if a group of creatives starts with the same information, each person's creative process will be different in some way. For example, I struggled with the fact that I didn't like structure, yet felt overwhelmed when trying to digest all the information I'd gathered to address the business and marketing considerations with creativity. I felt disorganized and inefficient, which left me panicked and tense as sand poured downward toward my deadline. I needed a framework to help me organize the content that would inspire my work—something that would allow me the freedom to take risks with the relevant information.

So while in my Competitive Strategy course at NYU one day, Direct Marketing 2012 Hall of Fame inductee Dr. Marjorie Kalter challenged any one of us to step to the whiteboard and offer a strategic recommendation. After looking around a bit, I stood up and what I've named the creative strategy framework is what came out.

CREATIVE STRATEGY FRAMEWORK			
Target	Facts	Feature/ Benefit	Message or Objective

Since then, I've used this framework to:

▸ Develop client recommendations for new-business pitches

▸ Uncover strategic threads that inspire conceptual ideas

▸ Use the threads as a basis for developing strategic documents such as creative briefs

▸ Organize my notes in a kickoff meeting

▸ Serve as a group strategy session or thought-starter tool

Here's how it works. The categories are composed of information that you'll usually get from a variety of places, including the client, internal briefings, the marketing folks, and your own research. It is helpful to begin the organization process of using this framework right in the kickoff meeting. After taking the time to research the brand, product, or service on your own, use the following three steps to populate the framework.

STEP 1: QUANTITY

Organize your research into the corresponding columns. List all possible target groups; fill in the facts on the brand, product, or service; tease out the features and corresponding benefits of the offering; and draft any communications messaging or client objectives. Don't get too bogged down in details at this point, just place all your research into the appropriate category. Try to exhaust each individual column of information within 45 to 60 minutes.

STEP 2: QUALITY

At this stage, you'll consider each element in each column. You're looking to eliminate irrelevant items through a series of questions or reword your content to become more specific. Have we fully defined the target segments in demographic, psychographic, and behavioral characteristics? Could we build a campaign off each fact listed about the brand, product, or service? Is that indeed the consumer benefit resulting from this feature? Does that message communicate the takeaway we would like the target to leave with? Have we recognized any additional opportunities beyond the objectives our client gave us?

STEP 3: PULL STRATEGIC THREADS

After populating this framework vertically, look for connections horizontally. I call these "threads." They may not be obvious at first. The value here is the unexpected connections that emerge across categories to help you find inspiration within order. Ultimately, you should end up with quite a few

A JUMPING-OFF POINT

It is important to state that the creative strategy framework is not a template, formula, or recipe—again, it is a framework to organize all the relevant information and use it as a basis to create from. With order, I found clarity, which led to increased inspiration and risk-taking because I was on brand, on strategy, and on message.

viable connections you could discuss, generate concepts from, and defend like this:

Based on their need or behavior, this Target > Would be interested in a conversation centered around this Fact > Using this Feature/Benefit in the headline and copy to get their attention > To deliver this Message or accomplish this Objective (message or objective is your choice based on what is needed).

With a single strategic thread you can now write a brief, create relevant design concepts, write compelling copy, or make recommendations on how a client could move forward with this line of reasoning.

CREATIVE STRATEGY FRAMEWORK: COLUMN BY COLUMN

Target	Facts	Feature/Benefit	Message or Objective
▲ Define Targets in fragments that state demographics, psychographics, and/or behavioral terms.	▲ Decide whether the job should be focused on the brand or a particular product or service within the brand.	▲ A Feature is a physical quality or tangible attribute that defines the product.	▲ A Message is what the target should take away from your brand communications.
▲ Look here for logical ways to create segmentation. You could look for differences in life stage or why the group would seek the brand, product, or service.	▲ Look beyond the brand's website for good and bad items to list here. Blogs and reviews will show any gaps between what the company says and what the customer is experiencing.	▲ Tangible features often have intangible benefits and thus these are written as a ratio. This Feature enables this corresponding Benefit.	▲ A client Objective usually begins with a verb: Convert, Drive, Engage, Build, Grow, Increase, Decrease, etc. by % among X target. Place both messages and objectives here so that you can give yourself flexibility to determine which is more important to focus on in your pitch or develop solutions that focus on both.

Using the Creative Strategy Framework

If, at this point, you are thinking about how you could use this framework with something you are currently working on, you can jump to the next chapter or begin using that framework to get started right now. If you'd like more of an overview of how to use the framework in general, continue on in this chapter. Remember, there is no right and wrong way to do this. The faster you find ways to apply the concepts you learn to your everyday life, the greater their value.

Putting the Tool to Work

If you need more context on how you could use the tool, this section is for you. As I mentioned, I've found the framework to be very versatile—it can be used in a variety of settings with a range of personnel. Here's a rundown of how this could help in various roles.

▸ If you are a **creative director/art director**, I've found that the process works best in a brainstorming or strategy session, especially when you would like your team to become more self-reliant. When you and the troops are locked in a war room with a whiteboard, allow your whole team to supply the content for each column. While hanging back a bit at the 30K-foot view, you can watch the leaders emerge and pepper in suggestions here and there. Mainly you're there to keep the discussion on topic, and over time your team will be able to present concepts that are on brand, on strategy, and on message. This technique allows the junior creatives to become more strategic and independent.

▸ In **agency environments with mixed teams** on a new-business pitch or answering a request for proposal (RFP), it's best for one writer to lead from the board. It goes faster this way, because most times people in that scenario are already familiar with strategy.

▸ If you are a **working professional** using this at a meeting, organizing your notes within the framework helps to identify any holes and specific questions to ask while still in the meeting.

BEST PRACTICES

You can see which methods work best for you and your team, but here are some best practices I've learned after years of implementing this framework.

▸ **Random is the order.** Expect to hop around in the process of populating the chart with information; you don't need to fill in the columns in any order. As stated earlier, you'll only get some of the information you need and you'll have to seek the answers to the questions that arise to fill in missing pieces. For example, in a new product launch pitch, you may have extensive information about the brand or service but nothing about the new target you plan to identify and suggest the client go after. In that scenario, you'll have quite a bit of information for the second and third columns—Facts and Feature/

Benefit respectively—but not a lot of product-specific history to pull from. When brainstorming to develop a new campaign for an existing client, the messaging, target, or marketing objectives may be clear upfront. It may be up to you to find a new insight about the target's values and zero in on a relevant feature/benefit or compelling fact that could move the needle in the work. The point is that you should populate the chart wherever starting makes sense based on the information you have at the time. Again, this is about finding the gold through connecting the dots that emerge across categories.

▸ **It's not set in stone.** Since the process of compiling all the information precedes the process of whittling down to the right information, the chart should be a working document.

▸ **Keep your eye out for potential barriers to purchase.** Your kickoff meeting will likely yield some client objectives and positive information about the brand from the client, but the client may *not* have included any negative information consumers have stated about their experiences with the brand. Every time a new consumer uses the product, it is the moment of truth, when what is advertised is either as advertised or not true. If the experience goes well, you may have just gained an advocate who will post a positive comment based on his or her experience. As you know, this is

the gold potential customers dig for when they Google your brand in their research phase of the journey. On the other hand, bad news travels at twice the speed of light in social media, where negative tweets or Yelp reviews can go viral. Therefore, when developing recommendations, it is imperative to find any gaps in what the company says about itself and what the public says about the brand experience. Be resourceful in where you look for reviews based on the target's existing behavior. Use any discrepancies or mixed signals as an opportunity to build solutions that address the problems.

▸ **The framework is only as good as the information you populate it with.** You know what they say: Garbage in, garbage out. If you and your team spend the time up front to populate this framework with well-researched, thoughtful information, the work becomes stronger because it is focused only on what is relevant. Even if you have many different teams working from the same framework, you could give each a different strategic thread or write possible areas to explore based on multiple threads. Either way, the content in the framework will ensure that none of the teams are on a tangent because they are all working with relevant information. Be discerning, and though you may have to give this a few tries, it will yield a strategic foundation enabling the creatives to take risks while remaining on strategy.

Turning Words Into Inspiration

The creative strategy framework ensures that you have all the information you need, that it's organized, and that the creative solutions are based on real facts, features, and objectives of the product, brand, or service.

1. First, list all potential targets, product attributes, brand information, features, and corresponding benefits.

2. Next, create objectives or messages that the target should come away with after encountering your communications.

3. After achieving quantity, refine for quality through discussion. Consider each element and ask, "Can we build a campaign on that?"

4. Pull out threads and use them to focus creative development.

(Additional resources such as my webinar Creative Strategy Framework: Keeping Your Creative Team On Brand, On Strategy, and On Message are available on the web at *www.mydesignshop.com/creative-strategy-framework-design-tutorial*.)

7 Getting Knee Deep

The Advanced Strategy Session

Delving Further Into the Creative Strategy Framework

If you've worked through a creative strategy framework a few times and are ready to get even more out of it, or if your job requires a greater level of strategic thinking and analysis, I've included additional information for you in this chapter. We'll consider each category in more depth and I'll outline the decisions that need to be made to improve the quality of the chart's information. Quality is key in each step and the discernment to filter what makes it into the chart will only come with practice. Only you will know what is right based on the problem before you, so in this section I'll focus on the steps after quantity. At the end of each section, I'll put the content into the context with an example to illustrate. Let's say that our design firm or ad agency wanted to go after an assignment for the Amazon Fire TV Stick.

Cleaning for Quality

Now that you've filled out the columns in the framework, let's take an in-depth look at quality. Look through the content and erase anything that really doesn't have relevance, even if it's correct or true. There is no one right answer to what should stay and what should go; these discussions are a matter of perspective. This is where discernment comes in. One creative sees gold where another sees nothing. The yes or no answer to the question "Can we build a campaign on that?" must be followed with a rationale in order to determine if the element should remain. Facts like "Apple was founded in a garage" could be relevant if the campaign had something to do with their brand heritage, but if it was a campaign about recent products, none of them originated in that garage so it wouldn't be relevant. Information like this could therefore be eliminated at this stage.

What you eliminate will always be relative to what you are doing and the client's goals. Take this time to adjust the words you've used or further align or clarify Features and Benefits. Focus on the word choice at this point. Think through each connotation to determine if this is indeed what you are trying to communicate.

Researching Your Target

So who are the people who need this product or service and where could you look to prove it with data points?

For instance, tech blogs could help with (qualitative) directional insight into the psychographics and behavior of cord-cutters. I'd then try to map these characteristics to segments developed by syndicated research companies such as Nielsen to add a layer of certainty. These companies have performed quantitative analysis to form these segments from census, surveys, and credit report data.

SEARCH SYNDICATED RESEARCH FOR DEMOGRAPHICS AND PSYCHOGRAPHICS

Search Google for "Nielsen, Claritas MyBestSegments" or utilize databases like Mintel, or get data points from eMarketer, a great resource for digital marketing analytics research, to help you get numbers and characteristics on your target audience. We can isolate one target and come up with many concepts to reach that one, or aim at multiple targets, or recommend viable but unexpected new targets. There is no one right answer, only *your* right answer and a well-reasoned argument backed up with the data as to why it's right.

▸ Tech-silvers, or older users who were cutting cable out of their existing TV experience

▸ Binge-watching cord-cutters who are light gamers

▸ Amazon Prime members with HDTVs

When thinking through your target, you'll want to determine what aspect of the target's demographic, psychographic, or behavioral characteristics are most relevant, or irrelevant. In this case, binge-watching and a decision not to pay for cable suggests high Internet consumption. The implications of this behavior could be the use of a variety of screens including smart TVs, smartphones, smartwatches, and tablets. This behavior may span male and female watchers and could be found in both younger and older prospects. As a result, there is room for recommending segments or creating personas if the client doesn't already know whom they would like to go after.

Remember our Apple watch–wearing grandmothers who were cutting cable out of their existing TV experience from Chapter 5? From this one sentence, we know that some people in our target group may be retired and on a fixed income, looking for ways to reduce their overall bills. We know that they've probably long been empty-nesters or are widows with grown children, so they have no need to cater to anyone other their own TV preferences. They own flat screens (possibly as gifts from their family members/children) because they are in the market for a device with an HDMI connection. They are very much tech savvy, and as evidenced by the Apple watch, saving money is more from old-school principle than need. They are New-York-City-subway-riding, up-and-down stair-climbing, healthy, active urban citizens.

This background sketch shows how important it is to find the insights that will inspire creatives or inform those writing the briefs that should inspire creativity. Without a well-defined target segment or segments, we don't have demographics (facts like nationality, amount of money, family size, life stage, location, etc.). Though this is important, I would argue that in this example, psychographics and behavioral attributes (things like values, mindset, attitudes, beliefs about spending money or technology use) would be more important than the demographics. This will always depend on the job. There are no one-size-fits-all rules.

LOOKING DEEPER

Let's look at each of our sample targets in more detail. "Binge-watching cord-cutters who are light gamers" says to me that this target skews younger, but are probably between thirty-five and forty because they had a cord to cut in the first place. "Light gaming" suggests that they will use what is convenient but may have grown out of being full-on console game players, or may have children whom they now purchase that type of stuff for. This segment is likely Gen X, probably skews male, and grew up with Atari, Nintendo, Sega, and MTV. The MTV part may seem insignificant,

but it is how we know that when they were kids, they had cable in their household and grew up with cable and therefore had a cord to cut as an adult.

Finally, "Amazon Prime members with HDTVs" gives no directional insight concerning demographics—which may not be as important as the psychographics or behavioral characteristics with this particular product, but this is a determination that you'll have to make case by case. We do know that they have late-model TVs and order things online. The Prime membership could allow us to assume they have a computer and an Internet connection, but we have no evidence on how much they order or how they use their TV. In a brainstorming session or pitch, I would suggest finding an element of information that would allow us to understand more about this Prime member with an HDTV. You could conduct your own research, which might include primary company-sponsored info, industry-generated secondary research, or our justified triangulated conclusions. This is the opportunity to find a new target, such as new Prime members who joined within the last six months with an HDTV. These people may be new homeowners (or could have recently moved) who had the money to purchase new stuff but just haven't settled in. To inspire the setting for our creative concepts or messaging for this group, we could look at their new life stage—as new homeowners or as being new to a neighborhood, having a fresh start or developing new memories, in a new place with new or old friends.

Facts

This column should be an exhaustive list of everything you can find or think of that is relevant to the brand, product, or service. This first step will determine the scope you'll be exploring in this column. If we're looking at the brand, we will then need to explore the heritage and the portfolio of products or services for something to build our work on. In some situations the client will determine the focus, or as a freelance project you can give strategic recommendations in the form of scenarios (see Chapter 9). Either way, doing your homework here makes the entire process easier because you'll have a full understanding of the brand—its pros and cons, its history, and its current position in the overall marketplace.

DIG INTO THE BRAND

The Facts column is going to force you to really study the brand, product, or service. Are the individual brands more prominent—such as P&G's Bounty, Cheer, Dawn, Puffs, Tide, Pampers, Swiffer, Luvs, Febreze etc.—or is it more of a master-brand sub-brand structure, like Kellogg's: Corn Flakes, Froot Loops, Frosted Flakes, Frosted Mini Wheats, Raisin Bran, Rice Krispies, Special K, etc. Understanding this company structure will give you insight into the approach they are using to manage the brand you are pitching and will help you formulate options—some that are in line with what they are doing, and some that depart.

If you are designing for a brand with multiple products, then you'll need to list their products in the Facts column. If you are creating for just one product within the brand's portfolio, you'll place general brand information in the Facts column. This will become important when we speak about features and benefits later and when developing the copy for the executions.

Essentially, you're looking for any and all information on the brand. Here are some angles to research:

- ▸ Historical information on the brand
- ▸ Brand perception in the marketplace
- ▸ Positive information on the brand
- ▸ Negative information on the brand
- ▸ Information from the brand's website
- ▸ Information about the brand from independent (and reputable) blogs
- ▸ Customer service ratings
- ▸ Any spoof videos
- ▸ Information about the brand's product lines
- ▸ Parent company information
- ▸ Brand partnerships or associations
- ▸ Sponsorship information
- ▸ Events sponsored by the brand

SPLIT UP THE WORK

If you're working in a team, try breaking down this column into tasks for several different people to research—one of you looks at the brand's websites and press releases; one of you looks at industry blogs and publications; and so on. Your goal here is to amass as much information as you can. What you are looking for is any interesting tidbit of information that could be the gold nugget that we could build a campaign on. Keep two things in mind:

1. This should be exhaustive and your inquisitive creative curiosity should really kick in.

2. You will not know what you are looking for but will recognize it when you come across something interesting while digging.

COMPANY HISTORY

This is the place to dig up and list everything factual you can find about the heritage of the brand, product, or service. You might find stories, or just bits of info such as when the company was founded. Did the brand have a doll in its brand heritage like Buddy Lee for Lee Jeans? Write it down and find out why. Was the product developed by 39 failures in the formula like WD-40 (water displacement, 40th try)? Write that down.

If you were serving a client with a long heritage, such as an Ivy League university that wanted to leverage its equity into building an online MOOC presence, you would need to be sure to delve into that heritage to find all the potential elements you could start the conversation with or build a campaign on.

HOW TO RESEARCH THE BRAND

To research the brand, go beyond the corporate website into places where you can find what people say about the brand versus what the brand says about itself: blogs, forums, etc. You'll want to learn about any negative or positive recent press or recalls in order to know what areas, approaches, or visual subject matter to avoid. In the case of the Fire TV Stick, I found out from several sales associates when I asked them which product they recommended and why that you can jailbreak it. What people are actually doing with the product is essential to understand because it may help you formulate your solutions in the context of neutralizing what the brand could perceive as a threat.

Having a wealth of knowledge in this column not only helps frame the creative approach, it aids the verbal setup when talking through methodology. You get the boardroom's attention when you can tell the story of the brand or product with information the client didn't give you. That's why the time and effort it takes to populate the Facts column is worth it.

FIRE TV STICK EXAMPLE: THE FACTS

In this scenario, we are focused on a product from the Amazon brand, the Fire TV Stick, versus the Amazon Prime service itself. If you were using this framework for a new product launch there may not be much history, but list whatever you find anyway. A quick search of the Amazon website, tech reviews of the Fire TV Stick, and user reviews would populate this column. Since this section is focused on quality of information, for demonstration purposes I'd recommend whittling down the facts to those that enable the behavior the target exhibited in the trend research. Facts like:

▸ The vast amount of content available on Amazon that includes video/entertainment/music/games

▸ Consolidated access to both an existing Prime Video library and multiple streaming services on their big screen

▸ Any specifics on the Fire TV Stick technology that enables faster streaming of content without buffering

The Feature/Benefit Column

We talked a lot about features and benefits in Chapter 5. Now's the time to use those skills. Remember to think of them as one-to-one propositions— one tangible feature connected to one intangible benefit. Again, quantity is the objective of the first pass, so list all features and corresponding benefits and then isolate the most important feature/benefit combinations on the second quality pass. Keep in mind that the same feature can enable multiple benefits. Write out every feature you think of. Then determine which are most important and what should be eliminated/consolidated on the second quality pass. When cleaning for quality, I've found it best to approach the research with a hunch and let the

information prove or disprove what I thought. For example, this hunch could be a point of view on what you believe each target segment is looking for.

This column is where you will be pulling inspiration to write compelling feature- or benefit-oriented headlines and body copy that would resonate with the target. Naturally, some of these combinations will be points of information and others will be what compels the target to buy. This will be determined by the objectives (awareness, engagement, education, etc.) as well as your ability to recognize connections between the target and the brand.

FIRE TV STICK EXAMPLE: FEATURES AND BENEFITS
Here are some features and benefits of the Fire TV Stick. These features range from information to imperative according to target behavior and preference (features are from Amazon's website at the time of printing):

Feature	Benefit
Amazon Prime Video library	Gateway to unlimited streaming "250,000 TV episodes and movies" (added value: free with Prime membership)
Amazon Prime Video library	Access to exclusive Amazon Original content (binging enabled)
ASAP technology	Uninterrupted entertainment experience (without buffering)
The Apps	"Netflix, Amazon Video, HBO GO, and Hulu, plus games, music, and more"
HDMI	Access travels with you

The Objectives or Messages Column

This column will house both the business objectives and the consumer-messaging takeaways. Make this easier by placing an O: or M: before each point to distinguish what's an objective and what's a message. This is where the flexibility of the tool comes in. If you are pitching new business, you could propose objectives to the client and build creative solutions around accomplishing those. Or, if you are working on a product launch or rebrand, you could develop and highlight the takeaway messaging. Let's discuss each in more detail.

PRIMARY AND SECONDARY OBJECTIVES

Try to determine your recommendation on what are the primary and secondary objectives for the brand, product, or service you are working on and why. You'll need a rationale if you are heading into a pitch to justify the overall strategy, tactics, and action plan you recommend. The 10-K statement, along with market analysis and competition, will help you build your recommendations.

NEXT-LEVEL OBJECTIVE CREATION

In the first pass of populating the chart, you could include general objectives (such as "increase sales"), but when refining the content, you'll want to be as specific as possible when stating the objectives (such as "increase sales by 15 percent"). Keep in mind that when you propose double-digit growth, you'll need to be specific about the metrics that you'll capture to measure this. (This is an undertaking you'd do after you've become very comfortable using this material or when you have a team member focused on this alone.) Your strategy to achieve this goal could be to focus on the behavior or life stage of the target when they move or upgrade. The tactics could focus on mapping this to the months or weeks with the highest sales numbers or on a new product launch. The action plan will have the specifics on what the promotion name would be (for example, Shift could be a metaphor for changing addresses or shifting from the old product to new ones) and how you would recommend that the brand implement the strategy. Visualizing this is what we would design to show in the pitch, and could include the logo or typography for the promotion and mockups of the event, in store displays, microsites, apps, or digital ads.

If the kickoff meeting or marketing team received a specific objective (such as "increase downloads"), the creative strategy framework will help you determine the most viable target segment. More advanced teams will be able to find out at what percentage the app is currently being downloaded and then use that as a benchmark to get even more specific about the objective ("we would aim to increase downloads 8 to 10 percent"). It's all a hunch at this point until we can prove these quantitatively based on research.

FIRE TV STICK EXAMPLE:
OBJECTIVES

To build more specific objectives, we may even need to triangulate these "awareness" numbers and the number of Prime members with Fire TV Sticks. This takes reputable information that may have to be cobbled together to be convincing. For example, we could find the number of Prime members from the 10-K statement or another source and layer that over Fire TV Stick sales. From there, the interesting question is how many of those members also have sticks. Since their existing Prime subscription would give them access to the Prime Video streaming, then it would also increase the probability that they would purchase media from Amazon. In this scenario, the Fire TV Stick is the razor and the media purchases are the blades. As we dig deeper, these hunches will either be proven or evolve based on the research.

If you are in a client meeting and you hear phrases that begin with words like Acquire, Drive, Build, Reduce, Gain, Engage, Retain, or Win Back, jot those down in the Message or Objective column. These elements are what we are being asked to accomplish.

Back to our example. An objective of a Fire TV Stick campaign could be to increase awareness and sales among existing Amazon Prime members with HDTVs.

1. First, let's discuss **awareness**, a.k.a. as many eyeballs as possible. What are the other opportunities we have within the Amazon Prime webspace to cross-sell this segment on a new product that will allow them to utilize their streaming experience within the context of their HDTVs? We could assume that developing mockups within the existing ad spaces and promotional spaces the prospects are already engaged in would be fair game. Our pitch could include Amazon Prime shipping box mockups, and promotional tiles within the Amazon Prime website ad spaces or within the context of the Amazon streaming app interface on the HDTV.

2. Moving onto **sales** now. When you look at these examples of how to boost awareness, we've chosen the type of execution we are proposing based on what we know about the target's behavior. We know they order from Amazon enough to subscribe to Prime. Therefore, we know that they have Internet access, purchase items online, own or rent in a particular area, etc. With a bit more thought and research on Amazon Prime ordering stats, we could further drill down our segments based on behavior and target those that have purchased a certain dollar amount or brand of electronics, and then determine the recency of their last purchase, frequency of the purchases, and monetary amount of those purchases. From there, we can determine what metrics we would seek to move the needle on. This enables creative people like us to develop executions based on increasing the frequency of the segment's purchase habits by a specific percentage or number. Drive sales with a targeted creative concept or message aimed at the recency of the last purchase— such as getting those who usually purchase a movie once a month to do so twice a month, or getting someone who usually spends a certain dollar amount each month to spend more next month. Since we are now drilling down to specific primary or secondary objectives, making creative recommendations based on the target's behavior and channels they pay attention in, we increase the probability of success for our client.

A second objective of a Fire TV Stick campaign could be to **become the preferred streaming device among binge-watching cord-cutters who are light gamers**. We can try to do that through education and research. We can assume that this segment also has high-speed Internet access, and binge-watches shows through services like Netflix, Hulu, Vudu, and HBO NOW. We will need to develop multiple channels within the campaign to address the various stages of the customer journey that the target will need to go through in order to arrive at a purchase. For example, this group may need a website that outlines in black and white the head math on features and benefits of each streaming product. An education objective could include information on how many apps one product has versus another one. Could the website have the ability to make recommendations on individual preference and suggest additional products to purchase? It is up to us to create concepts based on accomplishing these goals, utilizing the information we have on the target's behavior and purchase history, then selecting the appropriate channel to mention the features and benefits that are of interest.

When we are successful, we increase the probability of the customer tweeting about his or her new purchase and expressing preference through becoming an advocate. If our research determines that people find the process of researching exhausting, our creative recommendations could include a concept in a channel to simplify the decision-making process. If customers do tell a friend or two about the brand, product, or service because the creative concepts were developed in a way that facilitates sharing, it gives us an opportunity to convert some qualified prospects already interested but on the fence.

MESSAGING

So what are we saying to the target? That's messaging. Messaging is what you want the target group to understand about you and your product, brand, or service after watching the video, webisode, reading the poster, attending the event, seeing the ad, or using the app.

Remember that these are broad-based messages that the target will be able to glean from the visuals and verbal messaging in your work. This will be helpful when you have to direct a writer or are putting this together and thinking *but I'm not a writer*. That's fine; just communicate the idea here, and the scribe or wordsmith will polish it. Articulate the message clearly and then refine the way you say it through rewrites or getting a writer.

FIRE TV STICK EXAMPLE: MESSAGING

Other low-hanging-fruit messaging we can glean from the Amazon website could include things like:

▸ The vast number of movies available on Amazon to stream

▸ Original exclusive content developed by Amazon

▸ The streaming or processing technology that enables speed (no buffering)

More targeted messaging ideas will come about after you establish the target or target groups.

Think, *What will the brand, product, or service give me in exchange for what I will give them?* It's broader than quid pro quo. Companies give us free content or items in exchange for information about ourselves, discounts when we recommend the service to our friends, and reward points for keeping their payment method top-of-mind in our own wallets. Our attention and endorsement by tweet or video review are all forms of currency. In our Fire TV Stick example, there are free promotional episodes, Amazon original content, and the ability to access your Amazon content across platforms. Your target messaging should be based on the overall value proposition, which could be defined in various ways, including "The portal to vast high-quality Prime Video entertainment, music, apps, and games." Regardless of how you frame it, messaging should be focused on what is most compelling to the target (visually and verbally).

This is particularly important for a new service or technology, because if the perception is that it's too complicated, that would be a drawback. You'll remember the launch ads when the iPhone came out; the communications had to explain each detail or feature and its corresponding benefit to the user as well as the overall concept of an all-in-one, touch screen, one-button device (Ooh, what's an app, sounds cool).

As the product or service matures, copycat products enter the market, and the masses begin to adopt the product in its incremental changes; the next phases of the campaign or communications will have different objectives. For example, our Amazon Fire TV Stick example has three major players in its competitive set: Apple TV, Roku Streaming Stick, and Chromecast along with others, such as DVD players, game consoles, and smart TVs with app and streaming capability.

Categories and products mature, so that means that there will be increased storage space, faster streaming speed, a changing or increased number of apps and games (before you read these words). So the second phase of this campaign could be to increase the number of people loyal enough to upgrade to newer versions of the same product. If we do a great job on the initial conversion, we could get that business in the future as well.

Finding "Threads" in Your Framework

As we discussed in the last chapter, one of the framework's top benefits is that it allows you to visually connect your target, facts, features/benefits, and objectives/messages to inspire creative business solutions. These "threads" can use this basic framework—but remember, this is just a guideline and the threads do not need to read exactly like this.

Target	Facts	Feature/Benefit	Objective or Messages
Target 1 defined in a short fragment with demographic, psychographic, and behavioral data	Historical information about the brand	1 Feature enabling 1 Benefit	M: What Target X should take away from the communication
Target 2 defined in a short fragment with demographic, psychographic, and behavioral data	Information from blogs about the brand	1 Feature enabling 1 Benefit	M: What Target X should take away from the communication
Target 3 defined in a short fragment with demographic, psychographic, and behavioral data	Information from the brand website	1 Feature enabling 1 Benefit	O: Increase traffic by X%
Target 4 defined in a short fragment with demographic, psychographic, and behavioral data	Brand perception information	1 Feature enabling 1 Benefit	O: Convert Target 3 by X%

This target > would be interested in a conversation centered around this Fact > using the Feature/Benefit in the headline to get their attention > to deliver this message or accomplish this objective.

The statement doesn't always have to be written in this specific template. Just use this as a guideline and a way to make sure you've captured all the relevant information for a sound strategic foundation. Get in the habit of making it your own. In our Fire TV Stick example, this statement might read:

Amazon Prime members > would be interested in a conversation centered around consolidated access to both their existing Prime Video library and multiple streaming services on the big screen > using a headline focused on the Apps/Experience to convey a message focused more on experiencing the entertainment you're paying for versus spending time trying to access it in different places > for an objective of increasing sales of the Fire TV Stick among existing Prime members.

Next Steps

Keep in mind that the thread isn't the idea itself; it is a starting point on which to build concepts and visual directions. This tool helps me to ensure that the ideas I'm entertaining are all using the relevant information and goals.

▸ If you are writing from this stage, you could write a targeted brief knowing that the content is relevant to the goals, messaging, and target you would like to reach.

▸ If you are designing from this stage, look to the words in each column for visual thought-starters.

The Feature/Benefit column is where you'll break down what the product is and connect it with what the benefit is in the consumer's eyes. This connection between the product and the people that will use it is key, and if you understand the common values between the two it is possible to create strong connections. The "value proposition" (or what the brand offers the target in exchange for her money, personal, details, or attention) will be expressed in the headlines and body copy that come from this column. This is why it is so important to get the specifics right here.

Turning Words Into Inspiration

When looking at each individual category, ask yourself specific questions to determine what should be modified or eliminated.

Target

▸ Be sure that you haven't become so specific that you've drilled down too far and missed too many people. "Tech-savvy grandmas wearing red sweaters who have one grandchild and who live on the ground floor of a third-floor walkup" is too specific. Likewise, "Librarians who own HDTVs" misses so many people.

▸ Be sure that the target is actually a person and not a profession. Think tech-savvy middle-aged bookworms versus librarians. List people who exhibit behaviors instead of listing job titles to hone in on your target.

- Don't forget to consider B2C or B2B options as well.

- Remember that just because you are using a clown, or a grandma, or a deer in your creative work, it doesn't mean that you are only targeting clowns or grandmas or bucks.

The Facts: Product/Brand/Service

- Be sure what's in this column are the facts that you can build a campaign on. Think through the objectives of the campaign to determine how to address those specific needs.

- There will be and should be discussion and points of view concerning how best to meet client objectives. Don't let that ruin the flow. Try to settle these by asking why or why not and then move on.

Feature/Benefit

- Resist the temptation to write more than small fragments here so that you don't begin to write copy. Just state in the simplest terms what the benefit is.

- Be sure that each feature you list is an actual feature of the brand, product, or service.

- Have you listed two features instead of some sort of benefit that comes from the feature?

- Remember that the feature is most times a physical characteristic and the benefit is often an intangible result of that physical feature.

Objective or Message

- Be sure the objective is written as a verb and connect it to a target.

- If possible, drill down to how you would like to move the needle. Is this a brand campaign, or a promotion, or a pitch where you'll need to recommend multiple campaign ideas?

- Allow what you are trying to accomplish to determine what you recommend, but be strategic on the options you present. If you'll have at least three options, center each option on a different objective or message based on what is most relevant to your client's business. Be as specific as possible.

- When writing messaging, write what you would like the target to take away from the communications and not headlines, taglines, or body copy. It doesn't have to sound polished here. Let the wordsmith polish the words; this should be the essence of what needs to be communicated and not the exact way to communicate it. As Luke Sullivan says in his essential book for creative people, *Hey, Whipple, Squeeze This*, "Say it straight, then say it great."

- There is no rule that says you can't clean more than once—if there's a lot of debate, leave what's there and review it again in another pass.

8 Finding the Gold

Turning Data and Insights Into Creative Solutions

I was never good at the Rubik's Cube, but I remember the year my brother, cousins, and I got one for Christmas. Six sides, six colors, nine individual squares per color, and the ability to twist it left, right, up, or down. I was fascinated with the concept but it was just too complicated for me. I loved to watch my cousin Allen twist that thing. He understood how to get one individual square from one place to another in a series of twists and turns. And over time, I watched as he learned to get one of the six sides all the same color, then two, and so on until he solved it. It was awesome. I would soon learn to solve it as well, just not with the same strategy expressed in twists and turns. My method was simple: pop off the squares of color and snap them back in. Done. It was just not as fun and never as cool to watch. I still have respect for people who can twist that cube with deliberate intent, bringing order to all those variables.

The Twists and Turns of Strategy

In business, marketing, and creative problem-solving, clients choose our firms and agencies for the way we twist the Rubik's Cube. Our strategy. Over time, I realized that looking for the one "right answer" in a profession that thrives on imagination is the wrong approach. There is no one right answer, just *your* right answer and why you think it's right. There is only viable and not viable according to the resources available, objectives that need to be met, and the metrics to measure whether it's working or not. As a result, there are infinite solutions differentiated by the strategic thinking of the person twisting the cube.

All of this brings me to my friend Judy Abel, Vice President of Strategy at Method Savvy and owner/principal of 32 Degrees North. Judy's thought process caught my eye on LinkedIn one day when I was looking for a guest speaker for my graduate classes at NYU. Specifically, I was looking for someone with a greater understanding of how to best leverage strategy within the creative process. After reviewing her site I fired off a tweet, and many guest lectures later, I haven't come across a better strategic approach. Judy's ability to twist and turn strategic insights into actionable communications planning consistently earns my respect. I am honored to have her present her approach to strategic thinking here in her own words.

▶ Turning Strategic Insights Into Actionable Communications Planning
by Judy Abel

In my career, I have found that three strategic questions appear with some frequency and directly impact any creative output:

1. What are the real underlying beliefs or behaviors of our target audience and how can we connect with those beliefs and behaviors?

2. What is the best way to actually reach our target audience?

3. And, how does this strategy become real and concrete?

In some cases, these questions may overlap and in other cases they fall at different points in the conversation. Either way, I have found knowing how and when to address each of these questions is instrumental in creating strong creative work that answers clients' real business needs.

CASE STUDY 1:
FINDING THE RIGHT INSIGHT

In 2011, Nestle Purina decided that it wanted to re-launch its Pro Plan dog food brand in Latin America. Purina has made minor forays into the LatAm market, but this was going to be a concerted push to gain prominence in luxury dog food for the region. However, it was up against some serious competition. In Latin America, very few people buy luxury dog food. Those who do buy it are buying it on the recommendation of their veterinarian and generally buy whatever brand the vet recommends initially for the remainder of their dog's life.

Unfortunately, one of Purina Pro Plan's competitors, Royal Canin, had already made a deal with LatAm vets. If the vets in Latin America recommended Royal Canin, these vets would get a percentage of the sales profit. This meant that Purina could not tap into a key consumer insight—within this market, people not only value but adhere to expert opinions and recommendations. And it begged an additional question: If people ask about Pro Plan, will the vet still push them towards Royal Canin or will they be transparent about the positives of Pro Plan?

Luckily, research from the region demonstrated the latter. We now knew that, if we could get people to ask their vets about Pro Plan, it would open a transparent, honest dialogue and give Pro Plan a fighting chance. However, since we couldn't leverage the consumer insight around the societal value of authority, we had to dig deeper in order to understand our target's beliefs and behaviors around their dogs. To give myself some direction for my hypothesis, I wrote down some general questions:

▸ What are distinct ways people engage with their dogs?

▸ If these dogs were persons, who would a dog be in its owner's life (e.g., the best friend, a wacky cousin, a child)?

▸ What type of person would pay the extra money for a high-end dog food like Pro Plan versus feeding the dog table scraps or buying generic dog food at their local store?

In order to get answers to these questions, I started writing down my initial thoughts based on my experience or knowledge of dog owners. However, I didn't stop there.

My next step involved looking through Purina's primary research and my own secondary research. As I combed through the video of Purina's focus groups, I started to notice something interesting. People who fell into our target audience demographics across all the various Latin American countries were referring to their dogs as their children. Additionally, these were people who already had human children but were also elevating their dogs to a similar level. It lined up directly to my hypothesis and ultimately our key consumer insight—one of the main reasons people buy their dog higher-end dog food is because they view their dog more like a child and, as with a child, they want the best things possible for it.

Now that I knew the consumer belief we wanted to tap into, I needed to figure out how we could connect Pro Plan to it. Our research showed that people who buy high-end dog food in Latin America start buying the food when their dog is a puppy and stick with this food for the remainder of the dog's life. This meant it was essential to build a connection to these dog owners early in the dog's life.

Since these dog owners were essentially new parents, I decided that we could learn and adapt the best practices of brands that cater to new parents such as Gerber and Pampers. New parents need a network of support from doctors to babysitters to other parents. They are looking for expert advice, they want guidance from others who have been there, they want to meet other parents, and they want their baby celebrated. These were the areas that needed to be applied to Pro Plan's social media presence in order to provide the support these "new parents" needed. Our creative execution became a multifaceted "network of support" for new dog parents and allowed Purina to begin to make a mark in a difficult to break-into market.

CASE STUDY 2:
USING THE RIGHT CHANNEL

In 2013, the Partnership at Drugfree .org (formerly the Partnership for a Drug-Free America and later the Partnership for Drug-Free Kids) decided to create an integrated campaign to convince teens who are considering abusing over-the-counter cough medicine containing DXM not to try it. About 5 percent of teens in the United States annually are on the fence about abusing DXM to get high. Our research indicated an interesting trend. While a number of teens were on the fence about abusing the drug, they could be easily dissuaded once they learned about the physical and, ultimately, the social ramifications of the drug use. What we realized is that teens wanted the ability to "test drive" the DXM experience, not necessarily to jump directly into taking it.

Our clients loved the idea of creating an experience to "test drive" DXM abuse. The next question centered on channel usage. We all agreed that an integrated digital experience was the best and most impactful place to get our message across. However, we didn't necessarily know what that meant. Were we going to create a social media–centric campaign? Were we creating videos? Were we creating an experience teens would engage with or was it more a piece of content we just pushed out? Did we want to ask teens to share the content via social channels? Everyone on the team had different opinions and different answers. Finally, we aligned on an idea. We would create a game called DXM Labworks. In this game, teens would use robots to experiment with the effects of DXM and see the ramifications socially as well as physically. But where would the game live? Should it be a desktop experience, a social media experience, or a mobile experience? Again, everyone on the team had different opinions.

I decided that we needed to answer the question by looking at research around teens' behaviors in each of these channels. Since we did not have primary research that was specific to the channel question and research on teens is generally expensive, I leaned heavily on secondary research sources. After spending some time reading through various sources, the answer became clear through these three points:

1. First of all, there was a trend of teens leaving Facebook. This does not mean that they were necessarily deleting their accounts, but they were becoming less active, especially as their moms, dads, aunts, uncles, grandmothers, and grandfathers were becoming *more* active. This meant a Facebook-based social media campaign was not the right location and other channels didn't have the critical mass to ensure success.

2. Second, most teens shared a desktop or laptop with their family members. Therefore, any site or game on this device would likely not allow for the privacy teens were craving.

3. Finally, I saw that mobile was a teen's "private sanctuary"—the place where teens are most likely to search for things they "shouldn't." Teens were using mobile devices to download free apps that allow them to explore and connect with their peers in ways that entertain them. And mobile gaming such as "Dumb Ways to Die," "774 Deaths," and "The Moron Test" were already places teens chose to spend time.

Using this research, we made the decision to develop a mobile game that built on the negative perception of DXM abuse and teens' fear of social disapproval to make DXM more undesirable. This game would be available through an app so it would not require an Internet connection. Additionally, teens who were curious but didn't want to download the app could see trailers of the game on their desktop via the iTunes store. Because of teens' concerns about privacy in the digital space, we made the decision to not ask teens to push any elements of the game via social media channels. If they did want to share a GIF of their robot, they could download it via their phone and share via their phone's operating system.

Because we truly paid attention to how teens were using various media channels and devices, the game was a massive success. It had more than 67,000 downloads in the first three months, surpassing our original goal by 557 percent with 1.3 million experiments completed and an average gameplay of over 7 minutes/session.

CASE STUDY 3:
APPLYING A STRATEGY

In 2011, Renaissance Hotels and Resorts were facing stiff competition in their category. Competitors like the W Hotels & Resorts had made enormous strides as leaders in lifestyle and luxury. Renaissance was desperate to catch up. It became clear that we needed to create a content strategy that would drive brand awareness and excitement. Ultimately, our goal was to make Renaissance increasingly relevant in the lifestyle space while building off the brand promise that "No matter where or why you travel, there's always something wonderfully new to be found." We had two defined targets with intersecting desires, the True Discoverers and the Armchair Discoverers.

1. The True Discoverers were defined as the people who find the latest gourmet spot *before* the food critics do, who are the first to tweet the latest breaking news, who constantly seek. They value being first to be "in the know."

2. The Armchair Discoverers, on the other hand, were defined as the people who enjoy learning about the latest interesting events through curated e-mails for those in the know, who are among the first to tweet the latest breaking news, and who may aspire to be true discoverers.

In order to make our strategy actionable, we needed to appeal to the two targets' intersecting passion points: making discoveries and sharing them. To do this, I took a deeper look at the brand promise. What I realized is that we had an opportunity to focus our content and experiences on four key themes found in the brand promise— destination ("where"), occasion ("why"), differentiation ("something"), and discovery and exploration ("to be found"). Each of these themes would be represented across every potential consumer touchpoint from key cards to concierge services to social media activities to our website. Our aim was to make people who engaged with the Renaissance brand feel excited and validated by creating a sense of secrecy. If they know Renaissance and what it has to offer, then they are living the ultimate proof that they are in the know.

By focusing on four key themes taken directly from the language of the brand promise, we were able to bring the brand promise to life and create a program that helped differentiate the hotel from the competition. This program provided a means to keep pace with their guest's nomadic curiosity by recommending new and interesting places and activities. Ultimately, Renaissance became the secret our audience was tempted to share. ■

Dissecting the elements of our content formula

ⓐ Destination ⓑ Occasion

"No matter where or why you travel, there's always something wonderfully new to be found."

ⓒ Differentiation

ⓓ Discovery & Exploration

Understanding the 4 pillars of our content strategy

ⓐ Destination	ⓑ Occasion	ⓒ Differentiation	ⓓ Discovery
The unique aspects of each hotel and city	**Why you are traveling** (weddings, meetings, events, etc.)	**The hidden gem** What's that "something"? What's that special thing about our experiences? Taps into our target audience's interest in being "in the know" about the emerging, the new, the latest and greatest.	**Encourages exploration both off- and online.** We want to connect with those who love to discover, who take pride in knowing something others don't. Taps into our target audience's love of sharing their latest discoveries with their friends and family.

Informational & Utility-driven ⬅ ➡ Engagement & Sharing

Type of interaction

Key Ways to Use Insight to Drive Creative Solutions

As you can see from Judy's thought process, the ability to formulate relevant questions, seek the answers to those questions, and delve into what drives the behavior are key to her approach to triangulating for transferable insights.

In terms of her process on aligning the channel with the target, taking the time to develop the right concept based on the insight is just half of the problem solved. It is imperative to allow the behavior of the target to inform where to speak. A concept that is rooted in a strong insight and tailored to the target's behavior moves the needle because relevance = response.

In making the strategy actionable, knowing how many target segments there are and what differentiates them was key to leveraging what they had in common on behalf of the brand. Judy helped translate the target's common values into touchpoints that the brand could manifest itself in to build a relationship.

When I look at these solutions and study how Judy arrived at each one, it reinforces my belief that there is only *your* "right" answer and why you think it's right. That said, you'll also observe the way Judy formulated her own questions and went about proving her assumptions because you will always be asked to justify why you think your answer is right. Her decisions were always driven by finding the right insight, choosing the right channel, and applying the right strategy.

Turning Words Into Inspiration

You will need to try and fail on your own numerous times before you can confidently arrive at presentable solutions like Judy has in this chapter— and I'm a firm believer that practice makes presentable. So if you've been looking for the right answer or have the expectation that it has to be perfect, let yourself off the hook and begin failing. Think about the project that you are currently working on, are about to start, or have just finished. Write down some questions that will help you dive deeper into the three strategic questions that Judy outlined in this chapter:

▸ What are the real underlying beliefs or behaviors of our target audience and how can we connect with those beliefs and behaviors?

▸ What is the best way to actually reach our target audience?

▸ How does this strategy become real and concrete?

After answering those questions, conceptualize, design and develop some creative solutions that bring the brand in contact with the target. This will take practice and you'll have to have patience with yourself as some initial solutions will suck, but this is all a part of making your solutions presentable.

Try this: Create tactics to talk about during interviews or pitches, find a breaking news event and create awareness for a relevant cause or charity using the event as an example of why the cause is important (e.g., March Madness, climate change, amyotrophic lateral sclerosis (ALS)). Create a hashtag and develop engaging tweets, curate or develop content that drives traffic to a charity committed to the cause or relevant website (examples: nwba.org, dosomething.org, alifestoryfoundation .org). As the story develops, develop your voice. Measure. See how many retweets, mentions, and people use the #hashtag over time. Repeat. Presto, you have just created a real-time case study that displays your approach to what's trending.

PART III

The Strategy Behind the Execution: Developing and Presenting Your Work

9 Beyond "Make It Pretty"

Positioning, Pitching, and Leading the Client

David Brooks wrote an article called "The Practical University" in the New York Times (April 4, 2013). The central thesis of his article made the distinction between "technical knowledge" and "practical knowledge." He argues that the physical university will have to contend with the rise of MOOCs (massive open online courses), which impart technical knowledge for free from a distance by becoming places where students learn what can only be absorbed in person. Brooks states, "Practical knowledge is not about what you do, but how you do it. It is the wisdom a great chef possesses that cannot be found in recipe books. Practical knowledge is not the sort of knowledge that can be taught and memorized; it can only be imparted and absorbed. It is not reducible to rules; it only exists in practice." This is not a new concept in our profession, and though he was speaking about the university environment, I see this applying to our day-to-day growth as professionals.

Learning the trade from a master dates back to apprenticeships in printing and aesthetics when you count assistants for masters like Michelangelo. I've been involved with developing this practical learning environment from professional training to the high-school level as an author of the curriculum for the first advertising high school in the country. My objective with this book is the same: to offer a practical professional development in the form of sharing my experiences, tools, and processes. These are designed to aid the development of your discernment to go beyond "just make it pretty."

This field is exciting and yet difficult to remain in because of the speed at which it moves. New devices, ways of accessing the Internet, and methods of communicating to prospects are being invented every day. What we can do, not where we went to school, matters. In this field of perpetual peer review, the ultimate vote of confidence from professionals in our field is having your portfolio selected from among the pile for the job. As my career has evolved over the years, I've continued to remain relevant by seeking to test my abilities through new challenges. I learn from the professional environment. Taking client problems and offering viable solutions for their businesses is where my professional growth is focused. Your ability to remain a viable expert will give you the experiences that validate your point of view in a field that values relevance over degrees. In this chapter, you will see some tools that could be a part of your new normal when asked to lead the client.

The Brand Ladder

All of the data you collected for the creative strategy framework gives you a wealth of resources for building a positioning statement. Before you write one, it's a good idea to first "ladder" your product or service (see Chapter 1). The process will help you extract insights to inspire creatives.

For instance, let's say you're going to build a brand ladder for Nikon. When you choose a camera, it's based on what you need it to do (communicate with social media, take color-accurate photos, etc.).

1. By now you know that you would first consider the attributes: the tangible features of the brand or product. For example, in this case, **attributes** could be a proprietary color technology or a Wi-Fi-enabled component in a camera.

2. Next, you determine the **benefits**: what the brand or product does for the consumer. These benefits are often intangible, but they can be traced back to a tangible product attribute that makes them possible, such as that proprietary color technology or Wi-Fi component. The benefit related to those attributes would be: allowing others to see from my perspective.

3. Finally, you'll want to identify the **values**—that's what a brand or product means to the target. You're looking for shared values between the brand and the target. If you can find shared passion between what a brand makes and what the target loves, those insights are the opportunity. For you to trust these values beyond any subjective qualitative hunch, they must be gleaned from sound primary or secondary research.

From the brand perspective, the value could be the passion for connecting people through shared experiences. That's the underlying reason why camera makers research and develop new technologies to capture and share those experiences in their purest form.

For the target's perspective, you'll need to find some sort of primary or secondary research, such as a survey on experiences, that allows the target to tell you what they value in their own words. The value in our camera example could be anything from capturing the moment to sharing it from their point of view, so you'll need to find out where photography enthusiasts hang out online and pay attention.

Once you have all of the necessary components—attributes, benefits, and values—you can use this as a basis to structure and create your positioning statement.

Use a Positioning Statement to Focus Creative Development

Once you as a designer, art director, copywriter, or creative services manager have a sense of the specifics of a project from a brief or your own research, it may be helpful to take a stab at a succinct articulation. Be sure you have first looked at the elements of the creative strategy framework from Chapters 6 and 7 and spent some time breaking down the product or brand features (attributes) and tying them to corresponding benefits. You can then add the relevant target values to build a positioning statement.

OUTSIDE EXPERTISE

Some of what I suggest here (research, data collection, etc.) may be outside of your expertise. That's okay. You may need to partner with a writer or a designer in order to extract the full value of the scenario analysis. Just like when a creative hires photographers or illustrators, you may want to reach out to other professionals to get the correct information. Lastly, the principle of going beyond the transactional designer-client relationship is what I'd like to stress versus the need to use these exact tools. Whatever your specific set of circumstances, having the discernment to be able to assess what is needed and apply the appropriate strategic tool is the point. However you need to do it, get to your right answer.

Positioning Statement >

For **target**, **brand** is the **category** that is the **point of difference** so they can **end benefit** because **reason to believe**

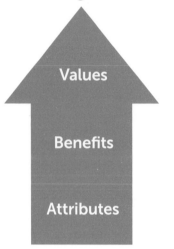

Values — What a product or brand means to the target

Benefits — What it does for me, the target

Attributes — What a product or brand is

Writing a positioning statement may help focus creative development and increase the viable options that are on brand, on strategy, and on message.

Here is a widely used and time-tested framework:

Framework for a Positioning Statement:

For (target), (brand) **is the** (category) **that is the** (point of difference) **so they can** (end benefit) **because** (reason to believe based on point of difference).

Target: Define the target based on demographic, psychographic, and behavioral characteristics.

Brand Name: This is whatever brand or product you are working on (Amazon, etc.).

Frame of reference or Category of business: BMW could be a car company . . . or the engineer of ultimate driving machines. The more creatively you can describe the frame of reference in ways that still apply, the better. An iPad is a tablet computer positioned in a differentiated way so that it is never described as a tablet computer.

Point of Difference: What can your brand or product say that no other brand can say? Qualitative and quantitative research should inform this point. An easy way to begin thinking about this is to imagine a consideration process where you had to evaluate and compare your client's brand with others. Try to find a way to sum up the point of difference with words that aren't generic.

End Benefit: This is where you state what this product does for the target. Qualitative and quantitative research should inform what is written here.

Reason to Believe: This cannot be an opinion statement; it must be rooted in the truth about this particular product or brand and its point of difference. Look into the details of the tangible brand or product features/attributes to craft a solid reason to believe, backed up with qualitative and quantitative research.

This is the one place where it's safe to throw away everything you learned about run-on sentences. Try to be succinct and make every word count, but be sure you capture everything you need to capture.

If your brand already has a positioning statement, be sure to keep it handy as you work on other campaigns for the brand. If you know this statement doesn't exist internally (either with the client or at your firm), try creating one when developing your

recommendations. Remember, the tool is only as good as the information you populate it with, so be sure to plug a specific feature into the reason to believe blank and a corresponding benefit into the point of difference blank.

EXAMPLE
In our camera example, the positioning statement could sound like:

For (creative professionals with an eye for capturing and sharing beauty), (Nikon) is the (digital point and shoot) that delivers (a window to their world), so they can (experience deeper connections through a shared perspective) because (of Nikon's 100 year history of developing new technologies that allow you to capture and share your experiences in their purest form, it's as if you were there). Again, I'm not a writer either—but if I can take a stab at framing this, so can you. Write something first and then you can judge it. It may take some time to become comfortable with the process of articulating strategy in this way, but this is how you unlock the difference between a one-time transaction and a long-term relationship.

Positioning is a process that involves in-depth research to articulate. *It is not a slogan—therefore, consumers would not see it.* It should be overarching on the brand level, where it would not be used short term or attached to a single campaign. This is where the impulse to be tactical is at odds with an approach rooted in strategy because it takes more than writing a witty line to create. You will no doubt find yourself in a situation or on a team where some on the team don't value the depth needed to formulate a sound strategy. If you are a junior designer or the scope is narrowly focused on your project, save this big-picture concept for when you are on a pitch team and have the ability to participate in this process. It couldn't hurt to ask the account team or an in-house marketing or brand strategist for this statement as well. Be tactful with these types of requests, because you don't want to spend all your time asking for things outside your responsibilities, but it will be clear when your job is harder because there is no strategy being developed. In that case, you can write your own to inspire the work they are asking from you.

A solid positioning statement will take a few drafts to get right, but once you've got it, place it at the top of the whiteboard or in the communications that you give to your team (after getting any needed buy-in from key players). It may take some time to become comfortable with the process of articulating strategy in this way before executing, but rooting your creativity in strategy makes for more successful business solutions.

Choosing the Right Channel for Your Creative Solution

After taking the time and care needed to make a clear, strategically sound positioning statement that's on brand, on strategy, and on message, you'll next choose channels that your target pays attention to. But that's only half of the challenge. Once you've chosen the right channels, the work of how to strategically position or differentiate a brand's offering begins. This section will teach you how to figure out what channels to use and how to craft a positioning statement to focus creative development.

When I say "choose relevant channels," this is for those of you who are in the position to make decisions on staff as creative directors. However, it is imperative that the whole team understand this in order to influence decisions in meetings, question decisions that don't make sense, or propose ideas to pitch the client. In some organizations, the design or creative teams haven't been invited to the strategy session or are not consulted at the very beginning of the project. As a result, the culture of your organization may define your role as executors (or they may not understand the benefits of injecting creativity into the initial business conversation). Whatever the case in your organization, the bottom line is that you may not have a say in where you communicate to your target. That decision may have already been made.

Even if that's the case, you can still understand the method used by the business and marketing folks making these decisions and can suggest additional ideas that are relevant.

COMMUNICATION OR MEDIA CHANNELS

Here is a topical list:

- ▶ Broadcast (TV)
- ▶ Web (video)
- ▶ Print (periodicals)
- ▶ Mobile
- ▶ Social Media
- ▶ Wearables (smartwatches and fitness trackers)
- ▶ Out of Home (billboards, phone booths, train platforms, bus shelters)
- ▶ Digital Out of Home (such as in Times Square)
- ▶ Point of Sale (counter cards, shelf talkers, end caps)
- ▶ Word of Mouth (this includes in-person referrals and forwarding links)
- ▶ Product placement
- ▶ Guerrilla placements

Simply knowing what channels are available doesn't equate to a sound strategy (this touches the key points from Chapter 3 on business objectives)—all of them won't make sense on one project. You'll want to choose the best mix of channels based on your knowledge of the target's media consumption and the business objectives.

Here is how you'll be able to propose additional ideas or ask the right questions to align brand, target, and channel.

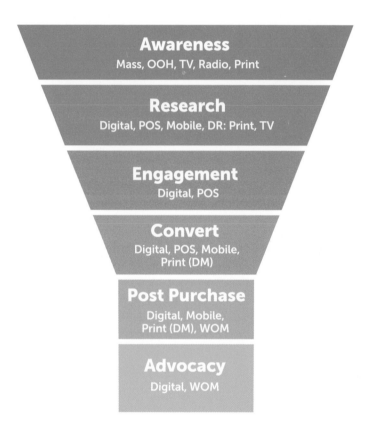

Awareness
Mass, OOH, TV, Radio, Print

Research
Digital, POS, Mobile, DR: Print, TV

Engagement
Digital, POS

Convert
Digital, POS, Mobile, Print (DM)

Post Purchase
Digital, Mobile, Print (DM), WOM

Advocacy
Digital, WOM

CONSIDER THE MARKETING GOALS
Choose your channel based on the marketing goals stated by the client. They likely fit into one of the categories in the purchase funnel: Awareness, Research, Engagement, Convert (Purchase), Post Purchase..., and Advocacy. For example:

▸ If your client or marketing department wants Engagement, you propose concept and execution ideas that will get them likes, tweets, reviews, and forwards.

▸ If the goal is Awareness, then you'll want to propose mass media touchpoints like Out of Home, broadcast, print, radio, etc.

Often, there must be multiple impressions or different forms of contact with your message for it to become top-of-mind and get some sort of response from a consumer. Each customer journey can depend on a number of variables. This is the objective of the funnel—to push as many people through the stages of the funnel, from prospect to customer to advocate. When you know what the suits are thinking, you can do what you do best—create engaging experiences in the appropriate medium.

For instance, an Amazon customer will most likely order stuff, and therefore the shipping box would be a great place for speaking to that customer (and all those along the way). The little yellow Minions with the big glasses were featured on the outside of shipping boxes with the Amazon Prime logo when their new movie was released. Since the customer is anticipating whatever he or she ordered, any sales messaging materials that ride along with what was ordered would most likely get more attention than the same thing sent regular mail. To take it further, if Amazon wanted to increase Prime memberships, regular Amazon customers would be the biggest opportunity to upsell. The ride-along postcards or brochures inside could make the customers aware of the service, make a special offer, or drive traffic to the website to close the deal.

FURTHER READING

In *Brand Portfolio Strategy*, David A. Aaker provides a wealth of in-depth specifics on creating brand relevance, differentiation, energy, leverage, and clarity. These will help you determine what creative approaches you may be able to take depending on what is best for the brand you are servicing.

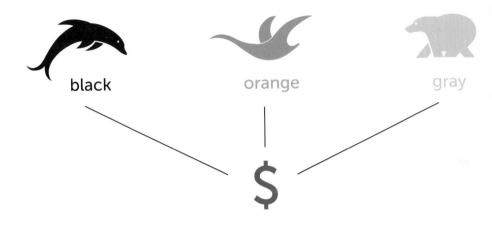

black   orange   gray

$

How to Build a Scenario Analysis

After you've done the research to create a brand ladder, written a positioning statement, and considered what channels are appropriate for your targets, you can start to think through your scenario analysis. This is a way to play out the potential risks and rewards of going with a particular option. As we discussed in Chapter 2, providing a tactical solution to a strategic request doesn't really solve the problem. Even if it does solve the immediate problem, it lacks the analysis that covers the scenarios the product or service will need to address in the short- or long-term future.

DOING WHAT WE'VE ALWAYS DONE
Let's say the client requested a new logo, and it is time for you to present your options. It's essentially a choice between the Black, Orange, and Gray options. In that scenario, the premise of the choice we present the client with is: Which one do you like better? Some would argue that no matter what they pick, the client is right because they are paying . . . but to them, I would say the premise of the argument is wrong because it doesn't include what's right for the target on behalf of the brand.

In this situation, you're offering three logo options for one price. There is no strategy behind the options; they're just creative choices.

Instead of a standard tactical approach,
your pitch could look like this.

STRATEGIC OPTIONS

black **+**

Scenario 1
Business Objectives:
Marketing Objectives: **=** **$$$$$**
Positioning Strategy 1:
Channels / Format
Risks:
Rewards:

orange **+**

Scenario 2
Business Objectives:
Marketing Objectives: **=** **$$$$**
Positioning Strategy 2:
Channels / Format
Risks:
Rewards:

gray **+**

Scenario 3
Business Objectives:
Marketing Objectives: **=** **$$$**
Positioning Strategy 3:
Channels / Format
Risks:
Rewards:

This is essentially the one job/three design options/for one price model as it is currently practiced, and it doesn't guard against anyone offering better or cheaper design. However, offering strategy in the form of scenarios not only differentiates your offering, it leads the client by addressing the real business or marketing problem.

What we show here are three different options, all based on different strategic answers to the business and marketing objectives. Each option requires various positioning strategies, different channels, and a different scope of work, and thus has a different price point. This method helps you lead clients to smart business decisions by clearly connecting the target, product/service benefits, and business objectives.

The scenario analysis is where all your hard work culminates—the time you spent getting to know your target, learning the history of the brand, teasing out benefits, learning specific marketing objectives, building relevant messaging. Show the client that you are doing more than throwing options out there—you're building a strategic plan for the brand or service.

With this method, your action plan (the itemized list of details, resources, metrics, and phases you would suggest that they implement) is well thought out. No matter what the client chooses, you've increased the overall value of each recommendation on all sides because of your analysis.

Turning Words Into Inspiration

Turning all of your research and insights into actionable ideas is one of the key parts of thinking strategically. Writing a positioning statement and scenario analysis that capture the strategy behind your solutions will help you lead the client toward success in the short and long term.

▶ Choose relevant channels based on your target's behaviors and preferences combined with the marketing goals.

▶ The identity, tone, and values of a brand help make it recognizable.

▶ Consider the phases of the purchase funnel or customer journey and how to best meet your target where they are.

▶ In your positioning statement, be sure the point of difference, end benefit, and reason to believe are rooted in research and not opinion.

10 Where's the Map?

11 Questions a Creative Brief Should Answer

Sitting there with my mouth wide open and the brief in my hand, I wondered aloud in disbelief, "Really. I'm supposed to develop a rich media digital campaign for a rheumatoid arthritis drug and there's no target information in the brief." Sure, I could guess, but wow, why even go through the motions of having a brief if it's not going to be useful? As the new guy on this account I was the second art director on this campaign. My in-house competition had worked on this brand at this agency for a few years. Awesome. As I sat there without any guidance from the strategy guy or information on where these ads would be seen (or if the target even used the Internet in light of their pain), my grandmother came to mind. As long as I could remember, we all knew she suffered from severe arthritis in her legs but she never complained. She would state softly in between jokes, a day or so before it would rain, "Ol' Arthur's acting up again." We could tell she was visibly in pain almost all the time as she rubbed her knees, but it was especially clear on those days. She would describe the sensation as "It kinda feels like they're in hot water, they just burn."

From there I fashioned an insight that people at this point in their lives owned their situation. They were living with the pain daily and it was as real a presence in their life as their grandchildren. It was personal, persistent, and painful, yet they had accepted the pain and learned to live with their condition. That led me to the visual concept that focused on beautifully photographed details of the affected areas such as hands and knees. Though I'm not a writer, I wrote a few lines I designed as quotes focusing on a day in the life of those living with the pain. It's all I had and my rationale to this point won the creative director, as she thought about the nickname her grandmother had given some condition she had as well. After a few days of client deliberation on the agency's two recommendations— the beautifully designed ads from my in-agency competition and my simple campaign—they rejected them both.

Why We Need Briefs

You may be able to recall many situations like this one, where you weren't set up to win because of incomplete information. How many times have you had no idea what to do because the brief was either full of worthless information or so vague you were better off before you read it? I've been there myself. I'll reference *Truth, Lies & Advertising* author and account planner Jon Steel throughout this chapter. His take on the brief is the single best-articulated view I've seen in my career. On page 172 he states:

"There is only one reason for anyone to write a brief or engage in briefing a creative team, and that is to help make their advertising better (and easier to create) than it would be if they were left to their own devices. As such, it is a means to an end: the creation of a distinctive and relevant advertising campaign."

We will focus solely on the parts of a classic brief in this chapter. You'll find various tools that (combined with any given information from the client) will enable you to develop your own brief if necessary.

In chapter 5 of *Truth, Lies & Advertising*, Steel lays out three objectives that are the goals of a good brief.

"**First**, it should give the creative team a realistic view of what their advertising needs to, and is likely to, achieve. **Second**, it should provide a clear understanding of the people that their advertising must address, and **finally**, it needs to give clear direction on the message to which the target audience seems most likely to be susceptible."

Even if you aren't in advertising, this information is still relevant. Your design will have goals to achieve, is meant for a specific target, and will need to communicate visually and verbally. If you are given a brief, it should sufficiently cover the content I'll discuss. If it doesn't, you may have difficulty creating viable solutions to the client problem. This chapter will give you a guide to what clarifying questions you can ask to develop the brief you're given to a more complete state.

Different Types of Briefs

Each organization is unique in the briefing process. Each project's scope and objective will require unique considerations that will tailor a brief to a specific communications problem. That's why:

▸ A brand built from scratch will need a more comprehensive brief than an initiative from an existing campaign.

▸ A digital brief will have different language than an outdoor campaign brief.

▸ Design briefs may be different than advertising campaign briefs.

You've figured and experienced that much. I'll be talking you through the framework of the transferable portions of a brief and the information needed to solve any problem.

The brief is where the specifics of the previous chapters come together. When sitting down to write a brief, you'll need a clearly defined goal or goals, a narrowly defined target, and some insight into what the target wants.

1. How would you describe the product?

Adman Peter Nivio Zarlenga said it best when he stated, "In our factory, we make lipstick. In our advertising, we sell hope." This section must answer the question, "What are we selling?" both literally and figuratively. On the surface, it may be a hair-growth formula for men, and underneath the surface it may be liquid confidence. You can pinpoint underlying motivations using Maslow's hierarchy of needs. (See Chapter 1 for more information.) Using this hierarchy to describe the underlying motivation for buying the product will frame this in an interesting way for those reading the brief.

2. What is the assignment?

The assignment can be described in tactical executions, strategic approach, or exactly as the client articulated from the RFP. Decide what is best according to the situation, but what the client has set out to accomplish must be crystal-clear in this section. Articulate both primary and secondary objectives here.

It's a good idea to look back at the signed proposal and scope of work while doing this to make sure that scope creep hasn't hijacked the project. If this ends up sounding like way too tall an order, or if something is out of balance, it's best to clarify now. Detail any phases, additions, or subtractions in the client wish list as well. Be brief yet specific enough not to be vague. A thorough job in this section will help you tackle step 11.

SPEND TIME HERE TO AVOID OBSTACLES LATER

It's my experience that when you find out you weren't even in the ballpark at the presentation or encounter insurmountable baggage as a response to some visual approach, section 3 wasn't properly discussed.

3. What is the background?

After reading this section, you should have an overview of the context that the product or brand is experiencing. If you're working on a design or a campaign for a food company that has just had a product recall because someone was sickened, you need to know that. It will shape the mindset of those you'll have to pitch your creative solution to.

Find out how the client defined success in previous initiatives. Uncover why the product is being relaunched and what approaches fell flat when they were tried in the past. Save yourself big headaches and delve into the marketing or business history of the brand or product here.

This is also the spot to include a written analysis of the top three competitors. Doing so will help frame the product or service within the context of the client's competitive set. Is this a challenger brand or a leader in the category? Answer this with prose. Bullet points won't work at all in a brief. A random list of things about each competitor won't give you a real understanding of what aspect of your business a particular rival competes with. (Example: If your product is better but their service outshines that fact, this should be communicated.) Links to or samples of their existing creative solutions should be included for reference.

4. Whom are we selling to?

Spending time getting to know your target is so important. Once you craft target segments, you can begin to find directional insights embedded in their demographic, psychographic, or behavioral aspects. Your channel recommendations, benefits, and messaging will all need to connect very closely to your target. If your brief doesn't define targets clearly or completely enough, you'll find yourself struggling with all phases of the creative solutions.

Chapter 7 discussed defining target segments, and with those concepts in mind, let's think through segmentation. Remember, segmentation is dividing your target into groups based on such characteristics as demographics, the target's life stage, psychographics (the study of a target's interests, attitudes, and opinions), and the behaviors and actions a target takes.

After proving that the target exists and is viable through quantitative data pointing to their behavior, we then must warm up the cold data by painting a picture of the people the data represent.

Choose a character from a TV show, movie, or your family who would best represent the target and create a persona. (This is where all that time spent watching TV comes in handy!) For example, imagine if Phil Dunphy from ABC's *Modern Family* embodied your target: a middle-aged, married real estate agent with three kids. His quirky personality and house in the suburbs would make it easier when formulating a concept, visual execution, and media channel approach to selling him a car.

Or what if Wilma Flintstone was most representative of your ideal target when selling a point-and-shoot camera. You know that this married woman likes jewelry, owns her own home, has a car, and goes out with her neighbors. You'd know that she has one child and as a result would have many family and social events to capture, document, and share.

Choose three of your favorite characters from movies, TV shows, or cartoons. Who of the three would be best to sell a high-end Dyson vacuum cleaner, a tandem bike, or a laptop computer, and why?

5. What is the one main benefit of this product?

This is where you articulate the selling proposition unique to this product or service. Put yourself in the customers' shoes and determine what's in it for them. For creatives, the relevant part to take away from this section is that the client, account, marketing, and business departments are looking for visual and verbal messaging that differentiates the product from its competitors. It's obvious that consumers comparison shop to find the best value for their money; to help you articulate that, you'll need features and benefits. A feature is what a brand or product is. A corresponding benefit is what that product or brand does for its target audience. See Chapter 5 for more information on features and benefits.

When looking at your phone, its touch screen, front-facing camera, storage capacity, and network are all features. These features enable specific benefits such as speed, ease of use, a visual and verbal conversation, the freedom to take photos while listening to music, or the ability to make a video and upload it. It's important to exhaust all these features and identify the corresponding benefits to the target that those features make possible. From this exercise, your team will uncover how the product or service is unique from its competitors. Determine which single benefit is most important or relevant to the target.

Sometimes this will be obvious based on the objective the client is trying to achieve. When the main benefit is presented clearly, it becomes easier for a potential customer to determine how one product may be better than another.

6. What are the reasons to believe?

You should find focused selling points in this section. These should be tangible product or service features that will justify why someone should listen. Thanks to people like you and me, we all are bombarded with thousands of marketing messages daily. When the design of an ad or the concept gets your target's attention, you'd better have something true to say. Format will dictate how much more you can communicate past your one main benefit (think 30-second spots versus brochure versus website).

To find unbiased information, delve into blogs, reviews, and the social media conversations people are having beyond the company's website and press releases. These are great places to look for truth. Truth often presents itself in the form of a disconnect between what the brand wants to say and what people are saying about it. It's our job to resolve this tension with a creative business solution.

7. What barriers to purchase do we need to overcome?

Actual or perceived, barriers are things that get in the way of someone choosing the product or service your client is offering. In recent history, Toyota had a series of automatic acceleration incidents, and that led to several recalls. This was clearly a blow to the brand heritage and trust that Toyota built over the years. Doubts about reliability and trust in the technology became a substantial disincentive to purchase. In this case, the barrier was from within, but barriers can also result from larger shifts or the economic climate. Now that Toyota has done quite a bit of work to rebuild that trust, it's Volkswagen's turn to rebuild after its emission scandals. List these barriers briefly, but be specific. Identify them so that you can overcome them.

8. What is the net takeaway?

When a customer interacts with a brand's marketing message or uses the product, a moment of truth occurs. The brand or product either lives up to the hype or it doesn't. After the target consumer has come in contact with your design, advertising, or in-store marketing, what should he or she take away from that interaction? In the car example, the key takeaway could be to re-establish trust through the value, innovation, and overall quality that Toyota is known for. I'm interested to see how Volkswagen will rebuild. A simple and focused message presented within a well-designed experience over time will more than likely be remembered.

9. What is the brand position?

A positioning statement is a succinct articulation of the target, brand, business category, point of difference, and reason to believe. If your brand has a positioning statement, be sure to keep it handy. If you know this doesn't exist internally for the client or internally at your firm, you might need to try to write one yourself. See Chapter 9 for more information on writing positioning statements.

Samples of existing creative work should be included for reference in this section of the brief. The graphic standards or brand guidelines should also be easily referenced for tone and brand personality so as not to deviate from what's on brand.

10. What is the desired response?

The customer will move on if you aren't clear in your creative executions about how to take advantage of what you offer. Each brand is posturing for a share of the customer's wallet. All brands that want to retain their current customers or convert prospects into customers should make it easy for people to respond. Should your prospects call, click, visit, or all three? This will depend largely on channel, creative format, and product. Be specific in the wording of your call to action and be sure to allow prospects the ability to respond in multiple channels. Whatever it is in your situation, be sure it's compelling and clear.

11. What is the timing?

Be clear on how much time you have to come up with everything listed in the assignment. List any phases, and pad a day or two here or there. You want to stay on topic and spend your time thoughtfully.

Do What Makes Sense

Keep in mind that there's no one way to approach a creative brief or strategy document. You may or may not include every section listed here. When determining the content of each brief, ask yourself, "Does it make strategic sense to omit or change the order of any sections?" If it does, make the case for why and take a chance. Strive for clarity rather than uniformity. Though I've personally found value in this framework from my former freelance partner and St. John's University Professor Neil Feinstein, there is no template. If it's worth its salt, it's a custom-designed strategy coupled with tactics and execution every time. You'll need to look at your specific project or organization to determine the exact course of action.

As our field evolves, I see the opportunity for smart creatives to become partners with business and marketing practitioners. That partnership benefits designers when we engage in whole-brain problem-solving—part strategy and part execution. It doesn't have to be us against the business and marketing folks, and creativity doesn't have to be relegated to execution. The creative brief is one place to capture all of the necessary components of a strategic creative campaign.

Turning Words Into Inspiration

Think back to the failed opportunities you've been a part of, and isolate the ones where you failed because you didn't have a necessary piece of the brief. We all have them, and they are painful because we put ourselves into our work; however, if we can put our finger on what went wrong, these experiences will help us going forward.

▸ Make a list of at least three failed attempts at making a concept work and isolate what the missing element was. Did this fail because of a lack of understanding of the target or was it because the creative format was misaligned with the media habits of the segment? Was the benefit unclear or missing or the barriers left unstated? This type of reflection will help you recognize when you don't have what you need in the brief and give you the opportunity to ask for these specifics immediately.

▸ If you're currently solving a brief, how does the content match up to the previous 11 points? What does it do well and why is that helpful?

▸ Each brief, client problem, and culture will be different so it is critical to compare and contrast what isn't working and who to ask for the missing pieces. Ultimately, if you can train yourself to see trouble coming, you can set off the alarm for the team so it can be avoided if possible, and if not, at least everyone is prepared for it.

11 Matchmaking

Aligning Target, Channel, and Messages

Fifteen miles off the coast of Anchor Point, Alaska, in the middle of the Cook Inlet, is where dating advice from John the Fisherman is doled out. "When fishing for the halibut, guys, you'll need to wait until they commit to you before reeling fast and steady. When women are on board fishing, they understand this the first time, but us guys have no idea what I'm saying. So just remember, even though you may see the rod bend slightly, be patient and wait until they commit before reeling fast and steady. A bit later when we are fishing for salmon, it may be slightly more familiar to us guys, because when you get a nibble, you have to be quick to set the hook, or she'll get away."

Before long, John the Fisherman's advice on landing a beauty began to pay off. We caught a boatload of halibut and silver salmon. John made it sound simple for us but when I think about it, though, there was much more involved.

The halibut rods, line, and rigs were much different than the ones for the silvers. Halibut, being bottom feeders, needed a four-pound lead weight so that the bait sank straight to the bottom. The bulky reels, strong fishing line, and large circle hooks were needed to handle monster halibut that have been known to grow to 400+ pounds. We began our halibut hunting with half a herring (a small baitfish about the length of your hand) and then worked up to placing whole salmon heads on our gigantic hooks.

The silver salmon rod, reel, and tackle, on the other hand, was different in every way. For starters, there was no weight because the faster silvers were only about thirty to fifty feet down. The reels were lighter, rods were longer, and lines were thinner. The key for these fish was a ten-inch reflector on the line that twirled as we trolled along the water. We needed to be sure that the lines weren't too deep in the water since we needed to reflect the rays of the sun. This attracted the silver salmon to bite because it mimicked the motion of a wounded fish right to our artificial lures.

Connecting All Your Dots

After a long day of fishing, it became clear to me that in order to be successful in the water, we needed to align the fish's behavior with the right bait and equipment. The same is true on land when we are fishing for prospects or customers on behalf of brands. It is our job to align brand strategy, media planning, and creative execution with the target's preferences. When these elements are present, the conditions are right for a long-lasting relationship. Just as in fishing, the resulting connections between the brand and the target are not the result of chance. Research, hard work, and thoughtful consideration are what make them happen.

Matching Target, Channel, and Messages

In this chapter, we will discuss the media channels that bridge the gap between target and brand by delivering the message. But even with this knowledge, there are times when we get nibbles all day but can't get a commitment. In these failed connections, there were barriers that prevented us from landing customers. Barriers to trust from not managing expectations, barriers to communication from unspoken expectations or the wrong approach, and barriers to willingness from not meeting expectations. Just as I needed John the Fisherman to help navigate through unfamiliar territory, I've invited a few seasoned professionals to guide us in aligning the elements.

First, storyteller and brand strategist Barry Silverman will discuss the four foundational elements that help creative teams and strategy teams align. I was first introduced to Barry in his Brand Strategy course at NYU. Shortly after, Barry became my client when we began working together on a design project for an organization he was helping to develop a unified brand with collateral. From there, Barry and I became colleagues on the faculty at NYU and often guest-lectured in each other's classes. I'm proud to have secured his contribution to this chapter.

Then, senior vice president, group client director, and communications planner Andrea Waite Spurlock will discuss removing the barriers that exist between the media channel and creative execution that should connect the brand and the target. Andrea and I went through the Masters in Integrated Marketing at NYU as existing practitioners in media planning and advertising. While attending, we developed a working relationship when I helped work with her to develop a website for a charter school whose board she was on. Andrea and I were the only two in our cohort to be invited to join the Integrated Marketing faculty on graduation day. We taught courses focused on the alignment of media planning and creative campaign development, involved coordinated weekly topics, and culminated in a joint term project with corporate clients. It is a pleasure to continue that collaboration here in this format.

Aligning Creative and Strategy Teams

by Barry Silverman

Max sat around the table with several other designers and creative people that he knows in the industry. It was their regular Thursday night meetup and a number of topics were being covered, as always. Max began his usual rant about clients and long hours, but today he was also annoyed at a planner who was clearly "overstepping his ground." His inquisitive friends probed and Max proceeded to describe the "pinhead" who not only did a brief, but offered several execution ideas as well, almost as a mandatory. Max hadn't even had time to read the brief and this cavalier member of the planning team was explaining how he very specifically understood the brand and what this client was looking for, thus justifying his creative strategy. He also tried to explain how it really couldn't end up in any other place and felt he was making Max's life easier. Max received a bunch of nods and sarcastic smiles of understanding from his friends as they each told a similar tale of woe. Why couldn't the strategy and account teams just let them do their jobs?

Max's problem is not uncommon, and unfortunately I never believed there was a single solution. In all my years working in this business, I have never had an identical experience from project to project. As a "brand strategy professional," however, I have noticed a commonality with every creative director I have worked with: quality of direction is key and enthusiasm for an idea is infectious. Let's start with "quality of direction." It's important to recognize the modifier for "direction," which is "quality," the antithesis of "quantity." Creative people don't want to read endless drivel related to the nuances of the brand; they want to understand thoroughly. An important aspect of the briefing process is being able to clearly articulate four things:

1. The communication objectives

2. The brand essence

3. The consumer

4. The consumer's relationship with the brand

There are generally additional elements to a creative brief, but I'll focus on these fundamental elements. What makes them so important is that they are often the foundational elements that help creative teams and strategy teams align. The idea of *alignment between strategy and creative teams* is a critical step in the creative process and often overlooked. It's an internal process that is completely transparent to clients and consumers; however, that alignment can be the gateway to greatness. To achieve this synergy, the strategy team must have a deep understanding of these elements and be able to articulate them clearly.

USING EMPATHY TO UNDERSTAND THE BRAND

The creative teams must be able to develop empathy with the consumer and then translate that empathy into creative work that delivers the communications objectives. "Empathy" is the key word in this equation, as the creative team should feel the customer's needs and problems, and their spirit—what drives them. They should understand the role the brand plays in the consumer's life and the relationship that the consumer has with the brand. I once had a creative director tell me:

"Don't read me the brief; I can read it. Tell me a story."

I realized that his way of feeling empathetic with the consumer was to hear a story about that consumer. Storytelling can be a powerful tool to create "quality direction." Stories can bring the consumer to life and identify the opportunity or role the brand plays.

What often makes this exercise challenging is that brands can be complex organisms with many moving parts. They are fluid and not static. Agencies have built complex frameworks around their processes for developing brands. For the purpose of the creative process, I'm going to limit the discussion of brands to three core aspects:

1. Promise
2. Emotional benefits
3. Personality

(I am not including "Positioning" for now, as this often seems somewhat academic; in my experience, to create empathy you need to be focused on the core drivers of the brand, while giving enough depth and character to the audience and how they benefit from a relationship with the brand.)

A **promise** is important to understanding brands because all brands are promises. They are what the consumer can expect and how the brand will deliver. A promise is sacred. It's also very defining, as it speaks to the core essence of the brand and what kind of experience the consumer can hope to have. The emotional benefit is the outcome of the relationship consumers have with brands. We can think of it as the "Why," whereas the promise is the "What." For example, I might say that Target's brand promise is to democratize design or to make designer goods accessible to the masses.

The **emotional benefits** consumers get from shopping at Target are feelings of accomplishment, satisfaction, and importance, knowing they have found great value in a shopping experience and have had the opportunity to buy brands that may have seemed difficult in the past. The promise and emotional benefits begin to weave a very comprehensive story around the brand.

When you add the **personality** component, creative teams begin to understand the tonality and style of the brand and the way communications should feel to the audience. In

Target's case, we could say they are fun, exciting, and energetic. Their visual identity, color, topography, and advertising all support this personality.

From there, I need to help the creative team understand the consumer. This can be done in numerous ways, but there is one way that I have found that hits upon the important aspects of the customer to drive empathy. The goal is to create a persona with the following elements:

▸ **Description:** Demographic and psychographic details of the person.

▸ **Motivations and needs:** What drives her, what's important to her? What role will the brand play in her life?

▸ **Pain points/frustrations:** In the context of this brand, what problems does the consumer have that need solving? How is her life made better by interacting with this brand?

Once this information is detailed, the goal should be to describe the consumer's relationship with the brand. This can be done in a number of ways, but I have found it always best to keep it simple. Ideally, the strategist should reflect on the needs of the consumer and how the brand is solving a key problem. This can be done through thinking of the "enemy." The enemy is what the consumer is struggling with and clues us to how the brand can take on the role of the hero. I find it useful to think of this scenario playing out in a classic novel: The consumer is the protagonist who deals with villains of all sorts. A villain can be anything from weight gain to bad breath. The brand is the hero who saves the moment or the day. In a novel, the brand would be the good guy whom the protagonist begins to rely on to make life better. In this respect, the relationship between brand and consumer is one of reliance and of gratification. There is always a higher level of betterment that occurs when the hero appears. The villain is conquered and cannot rear its ugly head, at least for the moment. Sometimes the villain is cast off into obscurity as the brand has laid the foundation for a new path. Other times the villain is subdued at least temporarily.

A CASE STUDY: DOMINO'S
Recently I have been working in the fast food category and have learned a great deal about QSRs (quick service restaurants). For example, Domino's, a company that has seen tremendous growth over the last few years, has transformed their brand. A creative team needed to work on the transformation of this brand and understand very clearly the consumer's relationship with the brand and what the "enemy" was to effectively lead the brand through successful changes. Ironically, in this case, the enemy was the brand itself. Domino's promise for years focused on delivery; however, consumers began to notice flaws in the product. Basically, the pizza just didn't taste good, and a savvier and more skeptical consumer took notice in a big way. The enemy was the waste of money on a poor product. Domino's successfully converted its brand from enemy to hero by improving the product

and being very transparent about it with consumers. They admitted to their mistakes and vowed to deliver a better pizza. This strategy has paid off handsomely, as they have seen their stock price increase by over 100 percent in the last five years. They are a darling of Wall Street and sales have seen tremendous upticks as a result of this new strategy.

The key to aligning strategy and creative teams is recognizing a few fundamental things the groups must do:

1. Know the brand

2. Know the consumer

3. Understand the relationship between the two

4. Help the creative team develop empathy for the consumer

Once everyone has absorbed these rules, two things will happen:

1. First, the roles of the strategy team and creative team will be clearly defined.

2. Second, a synergy will begin to develop between the two teams as they work toward a common goal to meet the communications objectives. If this happens, people like Max will be telling different stories at their Thursday night meetups. The conversations will turn to how proud they are of their creative work. And they will preach the mantra that behind every great piece of creative work is a great strategy.

The bridge between the two teams is the creative brief and the planner's ability to tell a story. The brief may have any number of elements, but as long as the previous four things are covered, the brief becomes a vessel for the sharing of great ideas, which leads to great creative solutions. ■

Avoid "Us versus Them" with Strategy

As Barry illustrates, creatives feel boxed in when being told what to do versus being inspired toward creative business solutions. In this scenario, everyone wants everyone else to stay in their own lane. This is the definition of "barrier" when the way we work becomes the problem, distracting us from finding the solutions the client came to us for in the first place. There is no alignment between the strategy and creative teams. At this point, there is no chance of the team addressing the four foundational elements that help teams align because it's "us against them" in a *Game of Thrones*–style internal battle. This is the beginning of the end of the account and everyone's job if someone doesn't refocus the team on slaying the dragon and not each other.

Which brings me to Andrea Waite Spurlock, SVP, Group Client Director at MediaVest. Andrea and I met as graduate students, worked together on a charter school project as professionals, and continued our collaboration as faculty members in the Integrated Marketing program at NYU. Andrea's experience with connecting brands and targets through media will continue where Barry leaves off.

▶ Aligning the Media and Creative Message
by Andrea Waite Spurlock

Aside from the brand/product itself, the target audience is by far one of the most critical pieces of intelligence to the marketing mix, yet it is often the most ambiguous one. Within a day's time you can hear multiple variations, all of which mean target audience: target market, campaign target, strategic target, product target, buying target, design target, behavioral target, media target.

WHO IS YOUR ENTIRE AUDIENCE?
We like to think the target is identified during the product development, recognizing and delivering against an unmet need for a specific set of individuals who will deliver the most value. But that is far from reality—that is just product/benefit target. It tends to be uninspiring and doesn't allow us to drive differentiation. For instance: whitening toothpaste—people who want whiter teeth; anti-aging eye cream—women who want to combat,

protect, or correct fine lines and wrinkles. These are the end users. A dandruff shampoo brand can easily say their target is everyone with dandruff, but when you see the advertisements it is quite clear that is not the case. You can tell by the talent, the tone, the look, and the feel that they had a particular person in mind when they developed the creative work.

The first thing any creative should do is question the target audience on any brief.

- ▶ Has the client aligned to this target audience? More often than not the answer will be a shocking no.

- ▶ Are there any other important iterations of this target I should know of? Lots of times the target audience is a segment of another, broader audience. That context, the story of how they've landed on this particular person can be very insightful.

- ▶ Who is the media target? Yes, they are often different!

- ▶ Can you share more information on who this person is?

A brief may have a one-line definition of your target, and that is fine. There are plenty of arguments that support the need and productivity from smart and concise briefs. That said, it is important for the creative team to truly internalize who they are designing for and how he/she fits in the larger picture of the marketing mix.

Now, what do you want to know about your target? A lot! The more you can identify with them as a person, the better you can develop creative that speaks to them, and motivates them to action. You want them to have an identity. Who they are, what they do, their passions and motivations. This information can be sourced from a number of places. Some clients have internal resources dedicated to consumer insights who deploy quantitative and qualitative research to identify the most appropriate target. Other clients just provide the product target and rely on agencies for the deep-dive. This means over time, our target audiences will become more sophisticated and reliable.

Whether the target persona is defined by the client or the agency, ultimately it must inspire both creative and media choices. If you don't have this, ask for it!

While I was working on a large B2B technology company we collectively— client and agency partners—questioned the brand's target market. Like most B2Bs, they were simply defined as business decision-makers, i.e., CEO, CFO, and technology decisions makers, CTO. As you may suspect, these didn't inspire creatives or media. Our teams decided to reexamine our audience and, using the principles outlined in Geoffrey A. Moore's book *Crossing the Chasm: Marketing and Selling High-Tech Products to Mainstream Customers*, shifted to a segmentation based on the spectrum of technology adoption. From there, we built out humanized

profiles (personas). They provided a texture we all craved. This led to stellar, differentiating creative and a media plan unlike any other year. This level of collaboration also resulted in better aligning the media with the message . . . where the magic happens. For example, the brand had a bold print ad featuring a woman on a runway that we ran in print titles and websites that had never made it onto the plan, such as *Esquire* and *The New Yorker*.

The newly defined, inspiring targets gave license to the creative team to be bold and the media team gave the creatives the confidence that we would meet their match, placing the ads in new and more contextually relevant and targeted places.

Truth is, we should think about the target through the line, down to when we go to market. Certain nuances can make a difference. It requires us to be less rigid and more flexible and also use some good-old common sense and gut.

When I was working on a consumer packaged-good brand (CPG), I had an interesting debate with the creatives about something as simple as a logo. We were working on a household name CPG brand with 95 percent awareness. Some consider it a cult brand, given its history and the affection people have for it. The collective team—media and agency—were working hard on launching the brand's social media page. (Seems like business as usual now, but at the time it was something we were all spending a ton of time on!) The creative team was working on the page itself, but also some paid ads that would run on Facebook to drive followers.

When they shared the creative banners, I was surprised to see that they used images of a viral video we had recently launched. They thought that the lighthearted feel of the video fit the environment, and also thought we could maybe simultaneously drive views. First, we can't do both if we want to do either well. We had to agree that the core objective was driving followers, not video views. Next, the banners had a small brand logo. I reminded everyone that we will organically gain a slew of followers just because people like the brand. We don't have to work hard for that first batch. For these initial ads, think of our target as brand loyals. They will see the logo and see we have a page and like it. Done and done. Because of this, I asked that they just create a simple ad that had the logo and a call to action to friend/ follow us. The good thing with digital is that you can run a number of ads and let the results decide. Lo and behold, the "logo" ad significantly outperformed all the other ads. For our second wave, we agreed we would have to try harder. We skimmed the top already, now we had to convince people that they should follow a household brand.

LOOKING INTO THE FUTURE

Target audiences are becoming more dynamic every day as we move away from the "one and done" era, where marketers developed a segmentation analysis and refreshed it, without necessarily challenging the segments themselves, every few years. What is driving this, like most of the change in our industry, is technology. We are shifting from "claimed" data sources to "actual." Simply put, claimed is what a person says they do. Think of a person filling out a survey or sitting in a group answering questions. Actual is what we find out about people via technology, via cookies and individual IDs. The result is more accurate, behavioral-based data. For creatives, this will require creative ideas and executions that are more flexible, as media buys are more granular, quickly moving to being able to identify people at an individual level and understand where they are in the journey. Right now, we can serve creative solutions dynamically, based on a number of factors/rules. Honestly, the industry has not moved as quickly as it could because creative assets are not available.

OVERCOMING BRAND BARRIERS

Whether addressed as part of the target or in the objectives or business situation, one of the simplest yet impactful business inputs a creative should have is the brand barriers. What are a target group's host of answers to the question "Why are you NOT buying this product?" These are your brand barriers. One step further, once you have that list—and for some brands it can be long—the next thing to do is prioritize. Unless you have a massive budget, you typically can't solve more than two or three barriers.

A brief may not list barriers. They can be hidden within the objective, listed as the "challenge," or even found under an "insight" section. The best thing to do is pluck them all out and simply ask yourself: are these your barriers?

Some examples of barriers are:

▸ Aren't aware—not purchasing the product because they are not aware of it.

▸ Don't understand (education)—not purchasing the product because they are not clear on the benefits/don't understand usage/never heard of what the product is meant to deliver. You find this often with pharmaceuticals.

▸ Don't believe the benefit/brand (believability)—not purchasing the product because they don't believe the claim.

▸ Don't think the brand is for them (relevance).

This is not an exhaustive list, but you get the point. If the #1 barrier is awareness, then everyone, creative to media, is tasked with developing a campaign that drives awareness. That will influence the channels we prioritize and the creative message. Most people will argue that creative should only tackle one barrier in order to keep the content simple and single-minded.

If awareness is really more about reminding (recency) consumers to buy your brand versus the other, which is often the case with many low-involvement CPGs, where switching between brands is a major issue, then you can see why the secondary barrier is key. You may be tasked with creating a TV ad to drive awareness but simultaneously tasked to overcome a relevance barrier.

It is critical to understand the barriers by target audience because they do vary. You may find one segment's barrier is just awareness, while another's is more about relevance.

While I was working in China, a global pharmaceutical brand was faced with a laundry list of challenges as they were a Western medicine in China, and in China, TCM (traditional Chinese medicine) rules. We conducted primary research to better understand what we were faced with. As we suspected, we had barriers across the consumer journey, from awareness all the way to purchase:

▸ The brand had only been in the China market for a few years and had a limited media budget, so it was no surprise that awareness was low.

▸ Brand understanding was also low. This was because product format was a gel, which was drastically different from the other products in the market (patches).

▸ People did not believe the product claims that it truly was better than their TCM regimens.

The clients agreed our biggest barrier was awareness, which became our primary objective. As a result, our media plan skewed toward awareness-driving vehicles and tactics such as TV, out-of-home (a big medium in China), and online banners. The creative dramatized the usage, showing how to use the gel, and had strong claims on why this brand was better than others. In addition, we, the media team, also encouraged the brand team to activate against a secondary barrier. We believed TV was not enough given the very unique barriers we faced in China. We needed a one-two punch. With that in mind, we developed a plan dedicated to busting the education and believability barriers. It included online advertorials that talked about the product superiority and layered in a robust paid and organic search plan.

Today, more than ever, we need to constantly think end-to-end. Clients have trouble signing up for any sort of strategy without the tangibility of tactics. And the funny thing is, once we start talking tactics, we can begin to question our strategic inputs. ■

Turning Words Into Inspiration

The underlying message from Barry and Andrea is one of greater collaboration between teams, leading to greater connection between the brand and the target.

▸ We also learn from both our contributors that as creatives, we may have to go beyond the brief and ask further questions of the strategic teams to truly understand the target.

▸ Knowing the passions and motivations of the target personas we are designing for is essential to understanding how to connect with them.

▸ With knowledge of how to best align teams, the creative process can yield effective brand activation concepts that rely on the intersection of media channel, creative idea, and technology. For examples, search Arc Worldwide's "Beautiful Hair, Whatever the Weather" campaign for Pantene or the Geometry Global "Animal Instincts, Pet Condoms" promotion for the San Francisco SPCA.

▸ Andrea reminds us to be sure that we are executing on the objective, and at the end of the day we can test various options and let the results determine what ideas live or die.

Barry and Andrea have described what it looks like to partner with our business and marketing counterparts. To follow through on my opening introductions to this chapter: When Barry and I collaborated to deliver branded collateral work, it resulted in a beautiful final product and ongoing client for me. Andrea and I were able to deliver a website that addressed their registration needs and saved the charter school approximately $100K. When alignment of teams happens, creative business solutions are the result.

12 Sell Without Selling

Preparing Yourself to Present

There is an old African proverb that says "Don't teach a child not to play with fire, let the fire teach him." Clearly, the wise old person who said this was really giving us a metaphor for pitching creative ideas. As I look back at my career, I can definitively say that the fire has been my best teacher. Some of my earliest memories of being burned were in graduate school at Pratt Institute. Every semester, we were required to present and defend the decisions in our work. The process was called "survey." Every detail of each project would be scrutinized in a matter of five minutes, from type selection and design choice to craftsmanship and presentation. A panel of world-class design professors would judge each detail in front of the whole student body. It all came down to this pitch, and it had to be perfect.

Some spilled blood as they sliced through fingers to make comps. Others dripped with sweat while watching their work print in large format. Many shed tears as it became clear that the orange they selected on screen wasn't the same orange coming out of the printer. And then it was my turn. Survey had gone well for me in previous semesters, and I was confident of the decisions I had made in my work despite some pretty public disagreements about them with my advisor. I had written, designed, and photographed a promotional magazine as my thesis. The masthead design was a custom Spencerian script with guidance from my distinguished typography professor Tony Di Spigna (it took me two months to tighten the four-letter masthead sketch that took him two minutes to rough out). Despite the countless nosebleeds and the time and effort invested in the finished design product, my five-minute presentation couldn't have been worse. As I looked out into the audience while giving my presentation, this was literally the moment I realized I was giving a sales presentation to a design school audience and they weren't buying it. If you've ever been judged by art school eyes, believe me, a few minutes is more than enough time to spontaneously combust.

The Art of a Presentation

In a profession where each idea, comp, and thought has to go through countless approvals, rounds, and revisions, you would think there would be a more deliberate means of teaching the art of presentation. Most times, the verbal aspect of presentation is learned on the job using the trial-by-fire method, like the surveys I endured. Other times, the creative work is given to a client-facing account person who couldn't possibly present your work with the same conviction that you could. Our passion for the work is part of the gift of being creative. We are an emotional people. We're trained to channel our emotion into tangible concepts using words and pictures that achieve client objectives. Yet most of us aren't actively trained on how to manage those emotions in the context of a presentation. We walk into a room full of people we've never met before and present something we've poured countless hours of love, creativity, and effort into. From the informal internal presentation to the formal new-business pitch, every designer knows pitching comes with the territory.

But knowing that the presentation is coming doesn't make giving it any easier. Most of us are juggling the stress and adrenaline of having multiple projects and deadlines. In an instant, the same emotions that enable us to create can become the worst stumbling block to finding the words to articulate what we've created. So when someone says "I don't like it," that can sound like "I don't like your nose." It takes active training and experience not to take rejection of our work personally because it *is* personal. On top of all the emotions, it's in the forefront of our minds that if the presentation is bad, our ideas get killed.

In his book *Perfect Pitch,* Jon Steel explores "'the presentation' not as just a single event but as a period extending from the moment the invitation to present is delivered, to the moment a decision is made. This period could extend over several months or even years." This view is a more holistic and comprehensive approach to client service that will require a whole lot of discernment and judgment.

So now that you've been given or done your research, defined your target, found a differentiated selling proposition, looked at all the relevant features and benefits and understood your campaign objectives, crafted the right positioning statement, written your inspiring creative brief, and had a briefing with your creative team ask yourself:

▸ How do you choose the right creative executions? What order do you present the ideas in? How do you set up or frame the presentation?

That discernment is what this chapter will be about. You'll get pointers on the process of organizing and presenting your creative ideas as well as how to deal with the everyday struggle of being a creative.

I've made a range of presentations over the course of my career. Some went great and others weren't. The main lesson I've learned in the sour pitches is that the context the ideas are presented in can actively hinder the work being presented, but it doesn't have to. Now that you've chosen the typefaces, images, and colors, presenting them in a way that will increase the probability of selling them is key. Mastering this skill will help you advance in your career, gain or retain more clients, and increase the probability that your work gets a fair shot at seeing the light of day. After all, this is why designers stay up working all night. Now, let's go sell it.

Establish Your Position

My professors at Pratt were world-famous design gods who either worked for Pentagram or Landor or were once partners with Herb Lubalin. We all knew who they were and why their opinions mattered. As you leave academia or gain more responsibility within a firm, it won't be as clear who's in front of you and vice versa. In business meetings, you'll need to get to the recommendation quickly and then explain or justify your thinking. Most business people or marketers don't know, understand, or care about the details of the creative process—that's our world. What they want from your presentation is a top-line understanding of why your approach is relevant and strategic—things that matter in their world.

Begin by answering their first two questions before they even ask them: "Who are you, and why should I listen to you?" The fact that they dropped out of Harvard to start a business, completed their MBA at Stanford, or inherited the family business got them to where they are. Likewise, get their attention by having a brief explanation or a few prepared sentences about why you—or your firm—are uniquely positioned to offer the right solutions to their business problem.

Here's an example I use: "Nine years ago, I stumbled into a strategy meeting and realized that becoming the 'creative who understood business' would differentiate me. This has helped me to inject creativity into solving business problems versus restricting creativity to the execution. 'Design plus business' experience gives me a complete strategic and tactical range of solutions, and I'm excited to share some insights with you today." Finding the right way to position your skills will take some work. Once you can articulate your value, it's a great way to introduce yourself and explain why they should consider your point of view.

Know Who's in the Room

Now that you've grabbed their attention, you'd better have a relevant point of view to share. Yet "relevant" is relative, so knowing who's in the room is essential. This will require some homework in advance—never enter a room blind. A few clicks in LinkedIn or Google should give you all the info you need to understand whether the person is an influencer or a decision-maker within the context of your project.

What's the difference? An influencer can have sway over the project, suggest a particular vendor, and usually will need to make a presentation to the person writing the check. As a mid-level person, he will need to manage the expectations of his boss as well as manage the productivity of the people who report to him. The person writing the check is the decision-maker.

As you present your creative ideas, know who your audience is and what their goals are. From there, you can recognize, extract, and weave the insights needed for their decision into your presentation. Framing the context of the ideas with business considerations is invaluable when needing to justify and defend the work. In business school competitive strategy classes, marketers are taught to read case studies from the perspective of the decision-maker. In doing this, they're then trained to develop solutions to the business problem using the information the boss had. This analytical tactic taught me to step into the shoes of a businessperson, use my discernment to sift through mounds of information, determine what factors are unimportant, and arrive at viable solutions.

GRAB 'N' GO

Regardless of who's at the meeting, your presentation should be transferable so that after you give the influencer your best in-person pitch, he can take the hard copy, slide deck, or leave-behind and pitch the person who can greenlight the project. The visual on each slide needs supporting copy or captions associated so that the rationale for the work speaks for itself when you aren't there. The worst thing you can do is bank on an audience member to remember what you said the way you said it when he's trying to sell it to the boss.

MATCH YOUR WORDS TO YOUR AUDIENCE

Remember, your business or marketing audience doesn't live and breathe design, so anticipate when an explanation will sound like "Nah-nu nah-nu nah-nu." This is particularly important for our digital brothers and sisters who understand the technical back end. Remember that you'll need to make explanations plain by speaking about functionality happening or not happening versus the tech specs if you want to be understood. When the time comes, be sure to use the business terms and concepts that your audience will understand.

Master the Setup

I remember being in presentations and realizing that I did one of two things: spoke too much before showing the work or didn't say anything before revealing it all at once. Both extremes are a death sentence for ideas. (Thank heavens the work in each situation was sound, because my presentation or context for the ideas was terrible.) Talk too much and you're like a commission-based sales staff at an electronics store. You always know the difference between someone "selling" and someone who took the time to understand why you came to the store. The latter person is meeting you where you are, asking questions to understand what you need to make the decision.

On the other hand, not saying anything ensures that you're about to be locked into a subjective opinion struggle with everyone in the room versus what works to meet the marketing objective.

On the way to gaining enough presentation experience, creatives will often waste valuable time explaining or talking through information the client knows all too well. There's no reason to recite the history of the brand to its own business or marketing team. They know it much better than you do. Ask yourself, "What part of this is a given? What do they already know?" Then approach your setup by offering *new* information. Try building your pitch on the implications of that history (e.g., how their history presents an opportunity to capitalize on a relevant emerging trend, or how this interesting tidbit about the brand's heritage will inspire a unique way to communicate to the existing customer base). Be sure your logic was inspired by factors relevant to the business problem they're facing. Think of how to leverage a particular behavior or mindset of the target, a feature or benefit of the product, a client objective, or a message that the target group should understand. Formalizing this part of the presentation will take some time, but it's worth it.

WHEN TO GO OFF SCRIPT

Business people like agendas, and agendas are helpful for organization. At the same time, when reading the room, know when to move in an unscripted direction toward the goal. But wait, this goes against all the practice/have a plan/ structure advice, you may be thinking. I stand behind all that; however, no plan always works and you'll have to read the room to understand when things aren't going to go the way you may have prepared for. (Think back to Dr. Kalter's story in the Foreword! Know the difference between going off script and going rogue.) Either way, practice makes presentable and if you are prepared to keep the objectives in mind, you have all you need to get to "yes" another way.

KNOW WHEN TO USE EMPHASIS VERSUS REPETITION

There is a difference, so be sure to differentiate when developing a way to reinforce a theme. When presenting, you'll need to look at the total picture to discern which is which. Set the timer on your iPhone and practice giving the presentation so that you can hear the points and revise where needed. Emphasize the themes throughout the presentation by highlighting the supporting points as they come up. This weaves justification into the presentation in a way that strengthens your overall position versus repeating the exact same information over and over again.

I can point to several reasons for the bumps in my thesis presentation at Pratt, but this was the main one: I went in without preparing, practicing, or thinking about what new information I was going to offer. Gone are the days when creativity for creativity's sake allowed for ideas that were presented as "cool" or "edgy." Design and advertising have changed from a purely idea-centric field to one that has to provide creative business solutions. Marketers now hold agencies accountable for their creative ideas, and as a result, success is measured in new customers and ROI. If you're injecting creativity into solving the business problem, you'll need to present the idea in a way that makes the audience aware of the business or marketing objectives you factored into this solution.

Set the Context to Anticipate or Avoid Negativity

The setup is also the place to try to neutralize negative client comments that could come in the feedback portion of the presentation. It's important to anticipate hot-button words, avoid negative connotations, and steer clear of previous failed approaches. Head off potential negative client comments like "It looks communist" after the presentation by framing what you've done before you show the work. "We were inspired by diagonals used in Swiss poster design, the color palette of Constructivist cinema poster designers Georgii and Vladimir Stenberg, and the visual symbolism of the strong figures used in muralist Diego Rivera's work."

Assuming that you've had a sound brief to work from, like the one I detail in Chapter 10, this approach gives sound strategic footing to show your creative ideas. The setup can be a powerful preamble that frames the reason that the concept or theme you're about to present is viable rather than an idea-suffocating eulogy better known as pre-ramble. Being orderly and strategic makes all the difference.

Pay Attention to Structure

Although I wasn't involved in any way with the long-running Apple campaign "Get a Mac," I'll use it as a familiar case study for how to structure your pitch. First, begin with the most relevant insight about the target you're trying to reach. This frames the reason that the concept or concepts you're about to present are right (form follows function).

Insight: "The larger market share of Windows-based computers makes most people more familiar with PCs. That doesn't mean they prefer them, though, because with that familiarity comes the headaches of viruses, uniformity, clunky user experiences, and crashes."

From here you can lead into what I like to call the "therefore." This is the bottom line or actionable conclusion from the insight.

Therefore: "If more people knew that the Mac alternative handled all the same functions while providing a cooler, easier, and overall more enjoyable experience, they would listen."

This leads us to the reason we are here in the first place: the verbal articulation of the creative concept or theme. It's tough to articulate a concept at first. You should be able to explain it in no more than a few sentences. If you can't, it's too complicated, and you'll need to simplify either the idea or the explanation. Remember, a concept isn't a description of the execution, it's the actual idea.

Concept: "The idea is to compare and contrast the differences between Mac- and PC-based platforms by personifying the computers and acting out the differences."

The execution is how the concept is being communicated. Think of the concept itself as the palm of your hand and the executions as your fingers. Depending on how big your campaign is, the executions are all extensions of the same concept. Executions live in media channels, and this is how campaigns are built.

The Manifesto: In the fourth edition of his book *Hey, Whipple, Squeeze This*, Luke Sullivan writes: "A manifesto is your brand's Magna Carta, Rosetta Stone, and Declaration of Independence all rolled into one; it's the halftime locker room speech given by the CEO; the words the founder heard on the mountaintop before bringing down the stone tablets. Reading a great brand manifesto should make you wanna run out and try the product. You should feel the brand fire in your bones."

You'll need to use your judgment here, but when launching a new product, relaunching a brand, or introducing a new brand, you'll need a manifesto. Sometimes this could be used in the launch ads, turned into a long-form YouTube video about the brand or placed in the retail environment. Use visual language so your audience can see what you mean.

Tagline: The campaign theme is explained through the brand manifesto and may often serve as the "period" in the piece. If the manifesto is the speech, the tagline would be the punctuation. It should sum up what's at the core of the brand in a memorable and differentiated way. This takes skill and much more in-depth study, so for more on writing taglines and creating smart creative work, consult my friend Pete Barry's *Advertising Concept Book*.

Execution: "TV spots, print ads, digital, or any other channel will focus on a different Mac feature such as banter about connectivity or an interaction around stability and, thus, give the reason to consider switching."

The benefit to the target group is a result of the feature in that particular execution. Features are tangible aspects of the product or service, and the benefits from those features are often abstract results to the consumer. It's the point of the execution and should be differentiated relative to competitors.

Benefit: "The benefit will be acted out between the characters to illustrate the ease of use, stability, connectivity, etc. (the things the target will do with the platform)."

Chapter 5 explains that the message the ads convey should be a plainly stated takeaway that the target audience should understand after coming in contact with your campaign in any execution.

Message: "A Mac does the same thing as a PC, just without the headaches and with a whole lot more fun."

The objective or goal of all this is one that would be given to you in the brief, or recommended as the agency/firm point of view if this were a pitch.

Objective: "Increase awareness: Make Mac computers top-of-mind when considering a computer purchase. Support the purchases of existing customers, and increase market share by convincing PC users to switch to Mac."

Again, though I wasn't in the room or associated with this idea pitch, this example shows that all of the necessary categories were well thought out and executed. Taking the time to write out *your* pitch structure provides clarity, organization, and flow.

Shut Up—The Work Is Speaking

Once you've given a clear strategic context, voilà, it's time to let the work speak for itself. Read any taglines or brand manifesto copy just before showing the visuals, one solution at a time (unless, of course, you've turned the manifesto copy into a part of the launch campaign executions). This will be the introduction to the rest of the creative solutions. Be sure that the first thing your audience sees is the concept that best embodies your idea (such as a manifesto). After you've read each element of copy, keep the audience focused on your presentation by turning over or covering any previous work before revealing the next solution.

It's also a good idea to comp print ads inside of the magazine, as they would be produced, or show any digital executions in their native habitat. Do this in addition to having the same presentation on a board. Only read what's in the work; if you did your job during the creative development and the setup, you don't need to do anything else. If you're reading a storyboard, read the dialogue as it would be on screen versus explaining the spot. Resist the temptation to add anything that's not part of the creative you're selling to the client. My time in the business yielded these insights—but only after I had been in the room as a creative for many years selling ideas versus creating the right context for the ideas to speak for themselves. You had your turn, now let the work shine.

PRESENTATION 101 TIPS

If you're presenting in Keynote or PowerPoint, be sure to present to the audience and not the screen. If there are multiple people on your team presenting, know who's advancing the slides and be sure they know when to advance them. And don't read the slides to the audience. Focus on highlighting the key takeaway of each slide in practice sessions. This is what you'll say as a voice-over while the audience sees the content on each slide.

After all of the work is presented, you can show all of the solutions and pass comps around the room. This will set the stage for client feedback in the last part of the presentation.

Now it's the client's turn to speak. This is the part where framing the work from the point of view of meeting the marketing or business objectives and trying to anticipate the creative minefield comes in handy. Hopefully, your setup and presentation will move the discussion away from the subjective critique or "like" and "dislike," and toward the more objective analysis of why an idea "works" or "doesn't work." If your client says the words "like" or "hate," replace them with "this works" or "this doesn't work" in your reply. You'll need to be sure to frame the conversation in such a way that you can get to the root of what makes the overall execution accomplish its objective or not.

Saying things work or don't work also lays the groundwork for you to draw your evaluator out by asking questions that seek to isolate the baby from the bathwater. If your client "doesn't like" the layout or concept, you can then ask if it's the typeface, colors, format, imagery, headlines, or connotation that they're reacting to.

WE'LL LOOK INTO IT (WINK)

You won't know what level of politics or trust you are walking into when presenting. If a client makes left-field comments even though you've done creative due diligence, consider saying "We can look into that" as a way to acknowledge the issue and then take it off the table for the time being.

We often hear vague feedback that leaves us more confused after a critique. If a client, creative director, or account person says "I don't like it" or "I like it," try to figure out why he or she feels that way. If you can put your finger on what "it" is, you can look into revising that element of the design versus starting from scratch because you didn't get specifics. I've seen so many great ideas die on the table because they weren't presented correctly and, therefore, had no buffer against the subjective black hole.

DO YOUR LEGAL HOMEWORK

The client's lawyer's point of view introduces yet another element that could kill your creative work. Sometimes there is no negotiation because of the legal regulations of some categories (such as financial or pharmaceutical). This is why it is key to ask if there are any legal requirements or restrictions upfront to consider while preparing your scenario analysis. Other times, you'll need to be sure to keep a laser focus on the business or marketing objectives so that the creative decisions remain on point instead of becoming diverted by the possibility of a lawsuit.

Fall Back on Your Research

Remember, all the work you have done thus far in the book has prepared you to deal with negative feedback. For example, if the client doesn't like the image you chose, explain how you picked that one because it resonates with X target audience and the product's X benefit. Think back to the threads you pulled out of your creative strategy framework and continually push the conversation back to the objectives everyone can agree on—the features/benefits/values—and you're more likely to make the conversation constructive and focused. If the discussion veers into subjective territory, drive it back on the road to the business or marketing objectives and terms you've learned so that you are speaking their language while getting feedback.

Enjoy Yourself

Last, try to remember to have fun. You choose typefaces, specify colors, and create concepts for a living—life is good whether you win the business or not. Present your ideas in an upbeat way that will increase the probability that you'll get past this next round, get the business, or close the deal.

Turning Words Into Inspiration

Presenting your pitch to a client is truly the culmination of all the work you've done thus far. When you've spent time and effort building a strong foundation based on strategy, you're much more likely to be confident, knowledgeable, and successful.

> ▸ Be sure to give new information, or frame what is widely known, in an interesting way or from a fresh perspective. Don't spend time restating information the room already knows.

> ▸ Don't talk too much while you show the actual creative pieces. Let your work speak for itself.

> ▸ When gathering feedback, keep the conversation focused on what works and what doesn't and try to tease out as much tangible information as possible. Steer conversations away from likes/dislikes and toward the strategic foundations of your solutions.

> ▸ Practice, practice, practice. Time yourself, plan out what needs to be said and what doesn't, and believe in your work!

PART IV

Stayin' Alive: Building a Successful Career

13 How to Take a Punch in the Face

7 Tips for Surviving As a Creative

Looking back, I can say that my experience at Pratt didn't prepare me for a job—it prepared me for a time when there were no jobs. A year after I was hired at my first gig while in grad school, I was laid off. The dot-com bust changed the landscape of the profession and I had to find a way to do what I loved, even when there was a year-and-nine-month recession in the industry. Pratt was an investment that has allowed me to flourish as a freelance designer/art director. Lessons like the ones you'll read in this chapter are at the heart of my belief that it's my responsibility to remain current and to take calculated risks in my career decisions. My layoff taught me that I had to determine how things would go with my career; I couldn't depend on an employer. Looking back, that period of extreme hardship and uncertainty was my most valuable time as a professional. The skills I learned during this time period would become the foundation I would build on two years later when I was hired at Brouillard, a (now defunct) specialized communications agency within JWT.

During my time at Brouillard, more and more existing clients requested digital services. One day, I spoke up and leveraged my own digital experience. My education and prior work experiences helped me open up a major area that Brouillard had yet to expand into. I understood the medium well enough to provide their initial requests. I proposed a solution that would enable my employer to offer a scalable web resource as part of its offering. The immediate client needs were met, but we offered no long-term, integrated web strategy or the capabilities to handle production at a profit. At that point I enlisted the help of my technology partner and good friend David Quintiliani to co-direct Brouillard Interactive. During our eighteen-month run, we saw the paradigm shift from print leading digital projects to digital driving the print projects.

Over the next eight months, David and I worked as a support for the agency's various functions, but our value was not reflected in our billable numbers. It became clear that the agency was unsure how to support this new capability. We anticipated this and tried to leverage our prior offshore relationships and experience working that way. Ultimately, we were overextended. The management was willing to embrace this new capability but was uncomfortable with outsourcing to my contacts in India.

Ultimately I decided to end my run at Brouillard. This decision was based on my desire to understand and learn how to overcome some of the obstacles we faced, such as advising companies on strategies for long-term digital success, managing an enterprise at an operational level, and integration of offshore capabilities.

Using Strategy to Further Your Career

There will always be someone who works cheaper and knows Photoshop better, so to stay relevant you must become strategic. I believe in developing the head and hands of a creative or designer in order to advance. Even after doing that, you'll still have to work with suits. So know what they are thinking when making decisions and develop your own judgment by factoring their considerations into your work. Even after you master this, you'll have to package it in some visual and verbal form of presentation, as we discussed in Chapter 12.

But then I thought, let me get some perspective on the long game of a creative career that I just don't have, since I still have a toe in my thirties. So I sought the advice of a veteran whose work I knew before I knew him. Enter Ron Berger, a Brooklyn native who started in the mailroom of the Carl Ally agency, became an award-winning creative, co-founded his own highly awarded agency that became part of Euro RSCG, and after 25 years as CEO, CCO, he retired as executive chairman of Euro RSCG North America (now Havas Worldwide). Ron has worked on numerous accounts and campaigns, including one you've probably quoted if you've ever said, "Time to make the doughnuts." His record of innovation includes launching Advertising Week as a former chairman of the 4A's and founding and creating the first advertising high school in the country, located in Brooklyn. Ron's credits are too many to name; who better to give advice on how to become a success.

▶ Career Tips
by Ron Berger

In 2009, I co-founded the High School for Innovation in Advertising and Media, the first public high school in the United States with a curriculum designed to expose students to the advertising industry.

The problem was we didn't have the curriculum.

Enter Professor Douglas Davis, who worked tirelessly as part of my advisory group putting together a curriculum that would lay the foundation for college acceptance, along with standards that would allow accreditation by the New York City Department of Education.

It was through this close working relationship that I got to know Doug well. He is a talented and committed teacher, but like any good teacher, he is always eager to learn.

So when he asked me to write some thoughts in this chapter for his book, it was easy for me to say yes. Helping creative people understand the importance of being better strategists, better marketers, better business people has been a decades-long passion of mine.

I hope you find this chapter helpful.

It's a list of things that over the years I learned, that helped me become a better creative person, a more successful Creative Director, and ultimately, a co-founder and CEO of my own agency.

1. Help clients feel comfortable with being uncomfortable.

I have been in so many meetings where powerful ideas were presented that clearly made the client nervous.

I remember a Volvo meeting in 1992, for example, where we presented ads that challenged the auto industry's commitment to safety. "The airbag is so powerful it's allowed an entire industry to hide behind it" one headline said, and then went on to explain Volvo's history of safety innovations, including the invention of the three-part seat belt, which Volvo never patented, because they wanted other car companies to be free to put those seat belts in their cars as well.

The client loved the ad, but was clearly nervous at its aggressive tone. I understood how the client felt, but also understood that research showed Volvo's safety leadership was being eroded by hundreds of millions of dollars being spent by other car companies trying to convince people that if a car has airbags, it's safe enough.

I used that understanding of the research, and suggested focus groups with car buyers of competitive cars to gauge reaction to the ad. And it worked. The client became more comfortable with being uncomfortable, the ad ran, and Volvo retained its safety leadership position. Key takeaway if you're ever in a situation like this: research can be your ally, showing the client you're open to feedback which can make the work a lot better and your relationship with the client stronger.

2. Bend but don't break.

Some of the great stories I heard when I got into the business were about creative people throwing tantrums if a client had the audacity to suggest changing a line or two in a campaign. One of the best was when after a client continued to critique a creative presentation, an agency founder walked over to the corner of the conference room, and began urinating on a plant.

The stunned client asked, "What the hell are you doing?!" The agency founder replied, "I'll stop peeing on your plant when you stop shitting on my work."

My advice: Listen to what the client says, then figure out what comments could potentially help, what comments won't make a difference, and what comments ruin the idea. Then you can sit down, and explain your thinking rationally and calmly. More often than not, a client will appreciate that you listened and agree with your point-of-view. And you won't need to replace the plant in your conference room. Or, more importantly, the client.

3. Awards aren't an end, they're a means to an end.

This may be pet peeve #1 about creative people. They present an idea they think is so brilliant, they're already building a new cabinet to hold all of the awards they're going to win. And they actually present the idea, pointing out how it will be a major award winner as one of its strengths. Yet they forget that the client they're presenting to sits in a cubicle in an office park outside of Cleveland, and has a hard time envisioning drinking bottles of rosé during a Grand Prix celebration at the Cannes Lions International Festival of Creativity in the South of France. Truth is, clients love winning awards, but hate being told they need to buy your idea because it will win every major award. Which leads me to pet peeve #1A . . .

4. Be more interested in your clients' success than your own.

Clients pay us a lot of money, but more important, they put their jobs, and their careers, on the line when they choose to work with us. And what do they get in return? Too often, creative people who put their own self-interest ahead of interest in the clients.

How do you stop doing that? Stop reading trade magazines, and start reading the *Wall Street Journal*. I did every day. Watch CNBC. I did every morning. I can't tell you how many times I read or heard something about a client's business, or a client, that enabled me to have a discussion with the client that showed I understood

their business in ways no other creative director could. These insights pay real dividends when you then present ideas that reflect what you read or heard about your client or its competitors. An article in the WSJ, for example, on trends in the fast-food industry led to "Eat Fresh" for Subway. An interview on CNBC with the CMO of Charles Schwab about how Chuck was still involved in the day-to-day business helped create "Talk to Chuck." And several stories on the sameness of German luxury auto design led to the campaign theme "Gorgeous" highlighting Jaguar's stunning design heritage. In all of these cases, drawing on outside reference points was invaluable in helping the client understand why these ideas were right for their businesses.

5. The best creative people aren't copywriters or art directors.

They're strategists, and directors, and designers. In other words, the best creative people can do everything. One of my former partners, Barry Vetere, was an art director by title, but was arguably the best strategist we had in the agency. He directed all of his commercials. And he was the voiceover for many of them. Google "Helmut Krone" and study the work he did for Porsche at Doyle Dane Bernbach— those were ads that were designed as elegantly as the cars themselves. Or look at the brilliantly designed campaign that introduced the iPod for Apple. You'll see design that brought to life the simplicity and joy of the product itself.

That's what the best creative people do: they capture the essence of what a brand and product are about, and bring it to life in ways that move people in amazing ways.

6. Clients rent ideas; they buy you.

I see this all the time: creative directors walk into a meeting thinking they have to sell this idea, or this design, or this TV commercial, or this ad, when in reality, all of those things are props that you should use to sell yourself. Sell how much you understand about the client's business. Sell how much you listened to the franchisees you visited to hear what's going on in the marketplace. Sell the insights you came away with after listening to consumer interviews.

Sure, you want to sell great work, and you should do everything you can to do that. But what I learned many years ago is that the most important thing you can sell a client is yourself. Why? Because when the inevitable happens in a year, two, or five, and clients decide they need a new campaign, you don't want them to also decide they need a new creative director to do it. All campaigns have a shelf life. You shouldn't.

Hopefully, the above has been helpful to you. I know it has been to me as it gave me an opportunity to capture some of the things I've learned over the last forty years in the advertising business, and pass them along.

7. But reading about my experience is one thing, understanding how to apply it is very different.

So let's give it a try. Here's an assignment that applies how I think creative people should approach opportunities:

1. Take a product you really like and use and create a brand strategy for it. Look at how it's marketed, its competition, assess the advertising, and write down what you like and what you don't like. Then develop a new brand strategy based on your insights. Who is the target audience? What need does the product fulfill?

2. Write a campaign line, develop a design and some visuals that capture the brand/product in a compelling way.

3. When you're finished, show it to some friends, or colleagues, and ask them for their honest opinions.

4. Revise your thinking based on their feedback.

5. When you're done, ask yourself this question: Would I buy this product?

Good luck. Enjoy. ∎

Skills You Need to Move from Beginner to Creative Director

Now that we've gotten the perspective from Ron, I'll add my $0.02 to the discussion on how to further your career.

WRITE

I'll start this by overtly stating something about the words behind the pictures that I've been emphasizing indirectly in each of the chapters in this book. Writing. I cannot stress how much of a benefit to my conceptual process it has been to articulate my thoughts in writing. It doesn't matter if you aren't a writer or whether you're the boss—being able to write a good concept, headline, or positioning statement will ensure that you are noticed in situations that require thinking. Sometimes this is the only way to test out the essence of the approach without getting bogged down in the details.

The rules of spelling, grammar, and punctuation are crucial to know if for no other reason than to recognize when to break them for the right effect (for example, Think Differently versus Think Different). The only way to learn this skill is to read the writing inside award-winning creativity. Get *Communication Arts*, The One Show, Art Directors Club, or Society of Publication Designers annuals and read the work. Be sure that the annuals are from the last five years because you'll need to remain familiar with what is now. I didn't mention websites because it is too easy to Google something that hasn't been vetted. You can then spend most of your time sifting through everything versus focusing on what has been curated by industry veterans.

ANALYZE

You must exhibit the ability to develop a sound written strategy from research.

The creative strategy framework in Chapter 6, positioning statement guidelines in Chapter 9, and the creative brief guidance in Chapter 10 are all examples of this. You may not need all of these tools at once but practicing them will help you choose what you should use and when.

SYNTHESIZE

Synthesis is the development of a relevant written conceptual execution created from the strategy (this includes headlines, taglines, body copy, brand manifestos, tweets, blog posts, and so on). The feature and benefit insights from Chapter 5 are an example of synthesis. The words of my mentor and Pratt Distinguished Professor Tony Di Spigna still ring in my head: "It's been said that a picture is worth a thousand words. In the hands of the right designer, a word is worth a thousand pictures." Whether visual or verbal, it all comes down to effective communication. And that communication must include key parts of the brand or service you're representing.

One of the best skills I've learned during the years is to admit when I don't know and then ask someone who does. It has helped me learn from those who have made decisions like the ones I'm needing to make, but even then, with their advice, I must still make the actual decision. Failure is a part of the process and even now I still make the wrong call every now and then. It's not the end of the world, and faking it till you make it is a waste of time. Ask if you don't know.

So I practice, and if you'd like more practice making creative decisions, you can purchase the classic *Harvard Business Review* "Case Study: Mountain Dew: Selecting New Creative (Multimedia Case)" by Douglas B. Holt, available here *https://hbr.org/product/ mountain-dew-selecting-new-creative- multimedia-case/503038-MMC-ENG*. Or, put your new learning to the test by turning to Chapter 15.

Turning Words Into Inspiration

Keep in mind that what it means to be a creative person changes with the speed of the new products and platforms created for consumers to use. We must always adapt, and challenge ourselves to redefine the role of a designer or art director as the business changes. What will not change is the requirement that we possess the ability to use sound judgment when making recommendations to our clients. The best recommendation is not always obvious, as we are tasked with selecting the best options to present from the multitude of directions that we develop when creating.

14 Dragon Slaying

Successfully Managing Fear

This is the story of the professor who had no intention of going to college. In high school, I was terrible at math and French but by my junior year, decided to go to a summer school math class on my own accord. I switched to Spanish to get my two years that colleges required at the time. I took the SAT three times to get the best score I could get in order to complete the college requirements. It would seem that I was doing this because I had the intention of applying to and attending college but nope, that wasn't the case for me.

I did all that to have the choice to go to college if I wanted to. I wanted to be able to say that I didn't go to college because I didn't want to, not because I couldn't have. I had no guidance within my high school, or familiarity with colleges except through family trips, an aunt, and a cousin who had gone to a local state college. And then I graduated from high school in 1994. I had my diploma but no plan for what was next. I happened to stumble onto a conversation about a top historically black college I had never heard of and went home and told my mom, "I'm going to Virginia."

I applied to Hampton University and got in. I was going to major in Fashion Merchandising, but that lasted all of the six hours it took us to drive from my home town in Lexington, South Carolina. When I went to registration and learned it was phased out, I thought to myself *I'll major in graphic design* because I didn't know what it was. The moral of this story is: try so you can fail and then succeed. Even if you don't have a plan, plan to increase your options because having choices is important.

Facing Your Fears

If you haven't guessed it, this chapter is about everything that you'll need to slay the dragon of fear when trying to enter or advance in the field. Now that you've been exposed to the language of business and gotten some tools and techniques for building strategy into your creative solutions, it's time to use those skills. None of it will do you any good if you give in to your fears. We all have them. Some of us are insecure about the fact that we didn't attend design school. Others are afraid to negotiate on money or scope of work, or to turn an opportunity down flat. Some are afraid of typography (and to that I would respond that you'll have to get over this one as soon as possible, period); others are afraid of learning a new coding language or software. The good thing about these types of fears is that they can be overcome with a little effort.

The really scary things to overcome are more big-picture: being afraid of failure, getting the "wrong" answer, working in a team, or presenting in public. These are fears that can't be avoided if you want to leverage the skills you've gained in previous chapters. Though there is no quick fix, I can relate to how you feel and wanted to offer some stories to let you know that you aren't alone. If I can do it, you can.

Dear Students: It's Not Just about Getting a Job

"The *worst* of you will get jobs." Distinguished Pratt professor and world famous typographer Tony Di Spigna did have a way with words—but on this occasion, these words confused me. "What? The *worst* of us?" I was busting my rump at 21 in graduate school, unsure if I could compete. When I think back, his words should have provided the comfort I was needing as I often thought aloud, "Design eludes me." But instead his words pissed me off, as I was engaged and confused all at the same time. That statement stuck with me, and later, as usual, I realized that he was right.

I didn't even have to apply for my first job in the field—literally, one came and found me after just one year at Pratt. Back then, everyone used a jobsite called Monster.com and that's where I was found, contacted for an interview, and hired. Up until that point, six out of seven days I walked around New York City without a dollar in my pocket, and overnight, I had a job in digital advertising with more money than I had ever had before. These were the days of the dot-coms back in 1999. I worked full-time in the day and finished my graduate degree full-time at night. Then the bubble burst.

A year to the day that the job came, it went. I was the first of my group of friends to be laid off. I saw it coming and three days later, I had a website up and was open for freelance business. It took a year and nine months to get a job again so I freelanced in the meantime. It was hard, but I fell asleep at night having applied to every single job posting on Craigslist and Creative Hotlist. I had a Master's degree from Pratt and yet had to work at the Gap to make ends meet. I'd call creatives at work and leave messages at 1 A.M. so that I would be the first message they heard in the morning. When they called back, they would leave messages while I was folding sweaters. I'd return calls on my break. Though that time was extremely hard, I had a few clients during that time and the experience came in handy when the market came back.

Fast-forward eighteen years. Now that I'm in a position to teach, I can't say the same thing Tony said to anyone I'm teaching. You are not walking out into the same field I walked out into. The worst of you will *not* get jobs. However, it has taken me all these years to understand the essence of what Tony was saying and I see that it remains true. Over time, as I became more experienced in the field, I realized he was really speaking about focusing on the quality of the work I was going to do after being hired and not on getting the job itself.

A while back I came across a *New York Times* article that piqued my attention ("What It Takes to Make New College Graduates Employable," *www.nytimes .com/2013/06/29/your-money/a-quest- to-make-college-graduates-employable .html*). In it the author Alina Tugend cited a recent special report by *The Chronicle of Higher Education* and American Public Media's *Marketplace* that stated, "When it comes to the skills most needed by employers, job candidates are lacking most in written and oral communication skills, adaptability and managing multiple priorities, and making decisions and problem solving." Interestingly enough, this resonated with my experience in school and my mission as an art and design educator. Clearly these items cited are the exact things design and advertising education seek to develop because, combined, they are the job description of any creative job.

So, how does it feel to have the exact skills employers say most students don't have? Though the worst of you won't get jobs, the rest of you have been trained in exactly what employers want. Yes, breaking in and sustaining a career in design or advertising is hard, but you have no excuses. If I can do it, then so can you. So the question I'll leave you with is, "Are you using the skills you have to create quality concepts and beautiful executions?"

The Root of the Fear

Here's my advice to people in different stages of their career who have various fears: **To the Professional:** You're afraid because you aren't using your passion to fuel the work. Align what you have to do with what you love to do and you'll never have difficulty with inspiration again. Find what you would do for free and channel it into the work so that you can pay the bills while pursuing your passion.

To the current student or recent grad: You're afraid because you're not using what you have. Many students call me a year after graduation afraid that their "degree is getting old," but I remind them that the degree doesn't have an expiration date. What does have an expiration date is their skills, their portfolio, and their confidence. If you're not practicing, it breeds the fear in your loss of confidence. So find the scenic overpass, mountain vista, coffee shop, painting class, or old classmate that inspires you and make something.

How and When to Use the N-Bomb

Another common fear that holds creatives back is the fear of saying no to a client in one way or another. It's a simple lesson, but knowing it can mean the difference between steering clear of danger and diving headfirst into disaster. Here it is: Know when to use the "n-word" with clients. Yeah, I said it. The "n-word." Now that I've gotten your attention, let me put this in context.

Early in the summer of 2014, I was contacted on LinkedIn by a very articulate prospect about a potential business relationship. I responded with thanks, as usual, and we spoke at length by phone about the work needed for a business idea he and his partner (a family member) had. In his initial e-mail, he seemed very clear on his business idea and stated the budget. Without any specifics, the stated budget for the items needed was fair enough. I had the product launch, digital, and strategic experience relevant to get the job done. The client was very formal—he called my references and spoke at length with three of them. After two weeks of vetting, the prospect was ready to meet.

He and his business partner then took me to a pretty expensive dinner, I signed a nondisclosure agreement, and they explained the business idea.

It was terrible.

I asked a few questions, one of which was about the business plan. He replied that the business idea was so simple, it didn't need one. This is when my red flags started going up. I should have halted everything right here and used the "n-word." Hindsight is 20/20.

I reasoned that I could help by benchmarking the company he had based his idea on and, using that company as a yardstick, explain why it worked for them and therefore why it wouldn't work for him. From there, I could give him the tools to tweak his offering and develop something original that would work. So I suggested that, wrote a proposal, and ensured that he would be able to determine viability from my research. I'm always clear that I'll make recommendations, but the client will be making the decisions. We agreed on my rate and signed the agreement; I did the research and presented it at another expensive dinner.

At slide ten of ninety-six during the presentation, I could read the body language but wasn't sure if it was impatience or confusion and asked for any questions. Our small discussion revealed a bit of both. He wanted me to just tell him what to do and trusted that if I did, we could be done with the presentation. This felt a bit like trust, but much more like the expectation that he had paid me to write a business plan. I assured him of the value in his understanding the viability research and the strategic tools I was presenting and continued. Something felt weird but I couldn't put my finger on it.

It was my intention to move on, having helped the client determine a lack of viability, and having given them the tools to reach viability in exchange for a fourth of the overall budget. Win-win.

Some time passed before the entrepreneurs called again, ready to move forward and hire me to launch their brand. I assumed they had taken the time to incorporate and tweak their idea using the ninety-six-slide presentation I delivered. I drew up a contract and after a month of back and forth on details in sixty-four e-mails (which included what was and what was not offered in the agreement, what was and what was not a part of my expertise, and even an option to have me project manage a cheaper team that wasn't mine, which I declined) and a check, I signed on to do the project.

I completed the first milestone on the schedule of the signed agreement, a creative brief, as per the signed agreement. I was five minutes into the call when something strange happened. The client stopped me mid-sentence and said, "Douglas, we are really disappointed in what we are seeing, we thought that we would be farther along than this."

I was blindsided. I had no idea what they expected of me. In the following conversation, I began to understand that after vetting me, paying me for a viability study, taking three weeks before contacting me again, sixty-four e-mails to clarify the subsequent agreement over three weeks and a 40 percent deposit to start the job, these guys didn't read the contract, or recognize or understand anything that they paid me to do. After all the explaining over expensive dinners, several presentations, and green lights, we were still here. All of this could have been avoided if at first sign of serious red flags, I had just used the "n-word."

I should have simply said no.

There are two morals to this story.

1. Listen to yourself when there is internal hesitation because it is best to avoid some situations altogether. And if you are sixty-four-e-mails-for-clarification clear, and still have a miscommunication, then

2. No has to mean no, even when you're telling it to yourself.

Different Kinds of Noes

Why is saying no so difficult for designers and creative folk? I don't have the answer, but it just is. Knowing that, it is important to develop the discernment to know both:

▸ When to give no for an answer and

▸ When no is not the final answer.

N-OOOH: WHEN TO GIVE NO FOR A FINAL ANSWER

As the previous story illustrates, saying no protects us from the projects that we obviously should avoid. No one can always do everything. Nor should they. And that goes for some jobs that would be more of a time suck than an enjoyable experience. I've worked under crazy, screaming creative directors and needed to raise my voice when telling them that this was my last day. Whether it is an unreasonable request from a client, the freelance project where they want something for nothing, or telling it to yourself so that you don't get sucked into it again: say no sometimes. It's for your own good.

Knowing when no *isn't* the final answer can be just as difficult to figure out. This is especially important for those still in design school or fresh out, trying to make it happen. I remember deciding that I was going to intern at the Smithsonian Institution after my freshman year at Hampton. I found an internship there and I applied in March, well before the May deadline, and waited patiently. After the semester ended in May without any word from Washington D.C., I called to follow up on my application. I was confused when I heard, "Sorry, you weren't selected for the program" on the other line because I had already decided that I was going to work there this summer.

So I went to D.C. anyway.

After a month of visiting the museums and looking for internships, I had two jobs within the Smithsonian better than the one I was looking at originally. One was a graphic design internship with the National Museum of American History, where I also shot and developed my own photos.

This is the first time I learned to set my mind and go get it. Hiding behind a computer in the comfort of your own home won't work most times, especially if the person you are e-mailing came from the old school. If the answer is no, sometimes you'll need to think through how you'll ask again to get to yes.

FORGET RIGHT AND WRONG

This is hard to do but important because though everything ain't for everybody, there is something just right for everyone. As a creative person, you have to figure out the right approach for the right people. With primary and secondary research, quantitative analysis, and deep knowledge of your target, there's only what's viable and not viable. Remember this when pitching to a client, or selling an idea internally—there is no right answer, just your right answer and why you think it's right. Be sure to base your conclusions on insights because everyone has an opinion but they will pay for your analysis.

The 3 C's: Learning the Wrong Lessons

Grades don't matter in what we do. See, here's mine.

```
  P R A T T   I N S T I T U T E          ACADEMIC RECORD        PAGE 1 OF 2
  BROOKLYN N.Y. 11205   PHONE: 718 636-3600       DATE: December 5, 200
  - - - - - - - - - - - - - - - - - - - - - - - - -     DATE DEGREE AWARDED:
     BASIS OF ADMISSIONS:                          MASTER OF SCIENCE   06/00
  Hampton University
  - - - - - - - - - - - - - - - - - - - - - - - - - - +
                                               + - - - - - - - - - - - - - - - - - - - - -
                                               |  PROGRM: Graduate Level
                                               |  MAJOR: MS Comm Design
            Mr. Douglas Q. Davis, Sr.          |  MINOR:
                                               |  CLASS: SECOND YEAR GRADUATE
                                               |  ID.NO:
                                               |  DATE OF BIRTH:
                                               |  MATRICULATED: 98/FA
```

COURSE-ID	TITLE	CRD TYP	GRD	CRD ATT	CRD CPT	CRD CALC	GRD PTS	GPA
	Fall 1998							
DES 619 02	TYPOGRAPHY II	I	B+	3.0	3.0	3.0	9.90	
DES 620 03	VISUAL COMMUNICATIONS I	I	B+	3.0	3.0	3.0	9.90	
DES 622A 04	COMMUNICATIONS TECHNOLOGY I	I	A	3.0	3.0	3.0	12.00	
				9.0	9.0	9.0	31.80	3.533
	CUMULATIVE:			9.0	9.0	9.0	31.80	3.533
	Spring 1999							
CG 626 03	ELECTRONIC PRE-PRESS I	I	A	3.0	3.0	3.0	12.00	
DES 621 04	VISUAL COMMUNICATIONS II	I	B	3.0	3.0	3.0	9.00	
DES 625 01	VISUAL PERCEPTIONS	I	B+	3.0	3.0	3.0	9.90	
				9.0	9.0	9.0	30.90	3.433
	CUMULATIVE:			18.0	18.0	18.0	62.70	3.483
	Summer 1999							
DES 607 A1	PORTFOLIO DEVELOPMENT	I	A	1.0	1.0	1.0	4.00	
DES 654 C1	INTERNSHIP	I	A	2.0	2.0	2.0	8.00	
DES 660 A1	DIRECTED RESEARCH	I	A	2.0	2.0	2.0	8.00	
DES 673 C1	TELECONFERENCING	I	A-	3.0	3.0	3.0	11.10	
				8.0	8.0	8.0	31.10	3.888
	CUMULATIVE:			26.0	26.0	26.0	93.80	3.608
	Fall 1999							
CG 622 02	INTERACTIVE MEDIA I	I	A	3.0	3.0	3.0	12.00	
DES 699A 02	THESIS/PROJECT	I	B	6.0	6.0	6.0	18.00	
HD 510 02	HISTORY OF COMMUNICATION DES	I	A-	2.0	2.0	2.0	7.40	
				11.0	11.0	11.0	37.40	3.400
	CUMULATIVE:			37.0	37.0	37.0	131.20	3.546
	Spring 2000							
DES 635 01	TYPOGRAPHICS	I	B	3.0	3.0	3.0	9.00	
DES 640 01	DESIGN MANAGEMENT	I	A	3.0	3.0	3.0	12.00	
DES 699B 02	THESIS/PROJECT II	I	B	3.0	3.0	3.0	9.00	
HD 506 04	CONCEPTS OF DESIGN	I	C	2.0	2.0	2.0	4.00	
				11.0	11.0	11.0	34.00	3.091
	CUMULATIVE:			48.0	48.0	48.0	165.20	3.442

```
        DOUGLAS QUEJUAN DAVIS SR
        DEGREE EARNED      06/00
        MS MASTER OF SCIENCE           Patricia Ciavarelli
        MS Comm Design

                                       PATRICIA L. CIAVARELLI, REGISTRAR

           TOTAL TRANSCRIPT:      48.0   48.0   48.0  165.20  3.442
```

NEW YORK UNIVERSITY

Name:	Douglas Q Davis
Birthdate (MM/DD):	
Print Date:	07/28/2015
Student ID:	
Institution ID:	
Page:	1 of 1

Send To: Douglas Q Davis

New York University
Beginning of Graduate Record

Degrees Awarded

Master of Science   05/12/2010
  School of Continuing and Professional Studies
    Major: Integrated Marketing

Fall 2007
School of Continuing and Professional Studies
  Master of Science
    Major: Direct and Interactive Marketing

Fundamentals of Marketing	Y50. 1000			3.0	B
Introduction to Direct & Interactive Marketing	Y50. 1010			3.0	B
Financial Planning & Analysis	Y50. 1030			3.0	C+
Statistical Measurements & Analysis	Y50. 1055			3.0	C

	AHRS	EHRS	QHRS	QPTS	GPA
Current	12.0	12.0	12.0	30.900	2.575
Cumulative	12.0	12.0	12.0	30.900	2.575

  Status: Probation

Spring 2008
School of Continuing and Professional Studies
  Master of Science
    Major: Direct and Interactive Marketing

Media: Planning, Buying & Analysis	Y50. 2010	3.0	A
Direct & Interactive Creative Offrs: Planning	Y50. 2020	3.0	A

	AHRS	EHRS	QHRS	QPTS	GPA
Current	6.0	6.0	6.0	24.000	4.000
Cumulative	18.0	18.0	18.0	54.900	3.050

Summer 2008
School of Continuing and Professional Studies
  Master of Science
    Major: Direct and Interactive Marketing

Ind Study/Internship	Y50. 3900	3.0	W

	AHRS	EHRS	QHRS	QPTS	GPA
Current	3.0	0.0	0.0	0.000	0.000
Cumulative	21.0	18.0	18.0	54.900	3.050

Fall 2008
School of Continuing and Professional Studies
  Master of Science
    Major: Integrated Marketing

Competitive Strategy	Y50. 1011	3.0	A
Database Mgmt & Modeling	Y50. 1025	3.0	B+

	AHRS	EHRS	QHRS	QPTS	GPA
Current	6.0	6.0	6.0	21.900	3.650
Cumulative	27.0	24.0	24.0	76.800	3.200

Spring 2009
School of Continuing and Professional Studies
  Master of Science
    Major: Integrated Marketing

Digital Marketing	Y50. 1035	3.0	A-
Operations & Customer Service	Y50. 2115	3.0	A-

	AHRS	EHRS	QHRS	QPTS	GPA
Current	6.0	6.0	6.0	22.200	3.700
Cumulative	33.0	30.0	30.0	99.000	3.300

Summer 2009
School of Continuing and Professional Studies
  Master of Science
    Major: Integrated Marketing

Advanced Digital & Emerging Media	Y50. 2100	3.0	A

	AHRS	EHRS	QHRS	QPTS	GPA
Current	3.0	3.0	3.0	12.000	4.000
Cumulative	36.0	33.0	33.0	111.000	3.364

Fall 2009
School of Continuing and Professional Studies
  Master of Science
    Major: Integrated Marketing

The C-Suite Perspective: Leadership & Int Mktg	Y50. 1060	3.0	B+
Brand Strategy	Y50. 2200	3.0	A

	AHRS	EHRS	QHRS	QPTS	GPA
Current	6.0	6.0	6.0	21.900	3.650
Cumulative	42.0	39.0	39.0	132.900	3.408

Spring 2010
School of Continuing and Professional Studies
  Master of Science
    Major: Integrated Marketing

Master's Project & Capstone Course	Y50. 4000	3.0	B+

	AHRS	EHRS	QHRS	QPTS	GPA
Current	3.0	3.0	3.0	9.900	3.300
Cumulative	45.0	42.0	42.0	142.800	3.400

End of Graduate Record

**ACADEMIC
TRANSCRIPT**

No, these are not my undergraduate grades (what undergrad design student who smoked, drank, and partied didn't make vast numbers of C's?). No, these reflect the best I could do as a serious adult, and I'm sharing them in order to prove this point. No one in the field has ever asked to see my grades or the three beautifully framed degrees that came as a result of these letters. Not once. Because they weren't the point of going to school. What employers and clients always want to see are the results of your education: What I can do. The way I think. My work. The experimentation and confidence that came from the hours of time I threw at problems to develop my work ethic. This is where I excelled, and no letter could represent the value of that. This is what levels the playing field and this is what you sell to employers who want to buy it from you outright by hiring you, or rent it from you through freelance jobs. It's the same for you.

So you went to the design program at the school without the name. Who cares? How's the work? Can you place your portfolio next to the people who did go to design school and blend in? In a profession where they'll hire the dog if his portfolio is better than yours, you'll probably want to start focusing on the quality of your ideas and not where you went to school. The reason you walked onto campus should be about the learning, not the letters.

Turning Words Into Inspiration

Remember, what people are buying is your judgment, discernment, and foresight. This intangible ability is a competency to solve problems. So when dealing with common fears, remember:

- Everyone faces fears in his or her career. Those who succeed have learned to overcome those fears with knowledge, practice, and confidence.

- It's not where you went to school or what grades you got that's important, it's what you learned and whether you can apply it to real-world business problems.

- Learn to say no when it makes sense. Don't let yourself get dragged into jobs that are dead from the word Go.

- On the other hand, know when "no" means "just try harder." Rejection happens to everyone. It doesn't define you unless you let it. Use the experience as a stepping stone on the way to something else. #getit

15 Portfolios Are Like Cartons of Milk

Word Problems from Relevant Practitioners

During my time at NYU, I honed the skill of articulating my ideas as a creative strategist. This has been a great asset in giving clearer direction to my creative teams and students, and as a result has helped me find an audience beyond the classroom. That's where my request to the design community of HOW Design Live attendees, my former students, and design greats comes in. I asked them to give an assignment representative of the problems they solve for their clients every day. The result is this chapter of relevant problems from relevant professionals, which with your application of the principles from this book should produce relevant portfolio pieces.

I want to say thank you to each of my collaborators from around the world, and say that I'm humbled at how giving you are, despite your busy schedules. You are the reason that many reading this book will be inspired to create a differentiated body of new work to achieve their goals, and this is especially important to those who are not located in a major city with a design community. On behalf of all those who will read your words, and be inspired to push past what they've done previously, thank you, thank you, thank you.

Freshen Up Your Book

This chapter could prove valuable beyond measure to your career. Now that you have acquired new information, there's a new problem: showcasing the new skills in your portfolio. No matter where you went to school, the quality of your ideas will level the playing field. Sounds easy enough, but most of us can't afford to quit our current jobs to focus exclusively on developing the portfolio needed to land a better position. Add the fact that job listings these days are written in such a way that they want to see a certain level of experience before trusting you with the position or project. But then how will you gain the needed experience if you don't get the position or project? To top it all off, even if you have a great book now, as fast as things change it may not be that great in six months. Portfolios are like cartons of milk; they have expiration dates. These problems are all too familiar to creatives and can make us feel trapped if not exhausted. If you've experienced any of this, I've got just the solution: fourteen more problems.

This collection of problems is designed to help you reapply your new skillset in the presentation of your work. This compilation of creative assignments—word problems—from creative professionals mirrors recent requests their clients have asked them to respond to.

Emely Perez is a designer and illustrator currently at J. Walter Thompson New York. Emely has won an ANDY's Bronze in branded content and her portfolio includes branding and identity for the 4A's Multicultural Advertising Intern Program (MAIP) and poster, game design, and illustration for the One Show awards.

ASSIGNMENT: Find an established brand that has been around for years but that has lost relevance among its audience. Construct a brand analysis to figure out what caused this turn of events and develop an action plan to counter these brand flaws. Create a comprehensive presentation that would walk the clients through your analysis, findings, and proposed solutions. ■

Sacramento-based brand enthusiast **Chemene Phillips** is a graphic designer, strategist, creative director, owner, customer, and soccer mom. Armed with a business degree, a background in IT, and a flair for design and marketing, it only seemed natural to combine the three. She takes a unique approach to her projects, ensuring the right combination of long-term business strategy, applicable technology, and effective design techniques.

ASSIGNMENT: Complete Rebrand and Visual Identity For Construction Industry. Company Name: Sage Construction. This includes a new logo, brand guidelines, tagline, positioning statements, printed and digital stationery (including PowerPoint template, Excel bid sheets, Word stationery, etc.), website design and development, copywriting, social media page presence and design, and business folder (print and digital versions).

The Brief: The logo has to function in single color, two-color, or grayscale across multiple channels in both large- and small-scale formats. This includes print items, digital items, large heavy construction equipment, hardhats, and work shirts. Its identity stands out from its competitors, and it should be memorable, impactful, clean, highly professional, and immediately recognizable. It can include a simple icon, but the typography must make a bold interpretation of the name. The target audience is age 25–75 and includes developers, project managers, property managers, land owners, general contractors, and public workers. The company should be positioned as a reliable resource that's been around for a long time for heavy construction needs. ■

Nick Matarese is the president and creative director of The Barn, a creative branding agency fully entrenched in the sports world. The Barn strives to create something Nick has dubbed a "franchise brand" for a professional sports team. His past clients include Disney, Adidas, Adobe, the AFL, Brute Wrestling, and several minor league sports teams.

ASSIGNMENT: Create a brand that not only shows the characteristics and personality of the business, but makes a personal connection with the city or community.

A sports team fails without a fan base. To create a true brand that will stand the test of time in the sports world, it not only has to represent the team, but should make the community feel like they are represented as well. You'll have to do your research for defining elements of the town or area and then combine those attributes with the mascot or marks of the team. For example, the Nashville Predators are loaded with local cultural influences: The name and logo reference a saber-toothed tiger, an animal whose fossils were found literally under the building where the team now plays. The secondary mark on their shoulder both has the stars from the Tennessee state flag and is in the shape of a guitar pick to reference the city's roots in music. Not only does the secondary logo represent the city's heritage in music, but guitar strings are inside the player's numbers and there is even a piano key design inside the neck of the uniforms. A great sports brand makes the everyday fan like the logo, and someone who understands the local references love the logo. ■

Jacob Cass is a prolific graphic designer who runs the popular design blog Just Creative, which doubles as his graphic design and branding firm. Jacob's clients include the likes of Jerry Seinfeld, Disney, Nintendo, and Powerade, and his award-winning work has been recognized worldwide; he was even declared the "top graphic designer in NYC" by the *New York Post*. He has a strong personal following on social media and his resourceful websites have been viewed more than 3.5 billion times.

ASSIGNMENT: Create a new logo + poster campaign for a NYC Broadway play. A new play is coming out on Broadway by the name of *Double Sided*. It's a tale of love and romance between a couple with the core message being that there are two sides to any story. Think of a rose . . . it's beautiful, but it also has thorns to harm you. Or a double-edged sword. Your assignment is to create a poster series that communicates these core messages. The poster should feature a logo/logotype for the words *Double Sided* and an instantly recognizable

image that can be used for all of the play's marketing. Think of *The Lion King*'s theatre poster: it has the large iconic lion image as the instantly recognizable image, and then the complementary type treatment for the words "The Lion King." Can you ace the king? ■

Intan Trenggana is an award-winning art director, currently working at a multinational healthcare ad agency. She graduated from CUNY's City Tech in 2010 and is expecting her MS in Integrated Marketing from NYU in 2016. Her brilliant design chops have taken her through a multitude of projects in various mediums—print, digital, even video games.

ASSIGNMENT: Growing up (professionally) in a pharma agency, I handle a lot of uber-niche medications—products that only affect one millionth of the mass population. That means that not a lot of people are aware of these products, much less what they treat. Pick a social issue—any social issue, doesn't have to be an illness. Your task is to build an awareness campaign around it. Social issues and illnesses you might want to consider:

▸ Transgender stigma

▸ Income inequality

▸ Hemophilia

▸ Alzheimer's

Look into your own cultural background: are there any taboos/preconceptions you don't find in your larger social surroundings? E.g., in Egypt, men don't reveal their mother's name for fear of being ridiculed. The act is considered taboo and has become a deeply ingrained part of their culture.

Short Brief: Budget is limited. Social awareness campaigns are usually backed by nonprofit organizations, which by nature don't churn out a crazy amount of money. So, consider your media mix carefully and have strong reasoning behind why you decide on those media.

The campaign has to be integrated. Be innovative both in your messaging and media choices. Consider your audience—how to best approach them? Is there an opportunity for sponsorships with other brands to help further the message? ▪

Michelle Muhammad is a Chicago-based designer, educator, maker, thinker, writer, and critic. Michelle is dedicated to using all of her God-given creative abilities to collaborate with businesses, nonprofits, educators, and individuals to help them design ways to achieve their goals.

ASSIGNMENT: My client works directly with at-risk, inner city youth in public schools across the country. Together we collaborate on designing curricula that teach social and emotional behavior skills, which help students cope with life issues while improving academically. During a recent conversation, he asked me the following questions: "How do we compete with the messages in images that surround our students? Can we still teach young people that 'decent living' or 'doing the right thing' is the best path to success when the images they see, and are most attracted to, tell a different story?" These days, people become paid celebrities overnight by degrading themselves in various media: The biggest fool becomes the greatest success. Impressionable young people perceive "celebrity" as an easier path to a fulfilling life. Students often approach my client with dreams of being the next big "star," rather than with strategies for pursuing a good education.

Brief: Find a local nonprofit that is grappling with a social issue that you care about and develop a counter-cultural ad campaign for an at-risk teen audience aged 13–17 addressing that issue. It could be a childhood obesity, sexual identity, or violence issue but it must resonate with the target and have a call to action that sends them to an engaging digital experience that offers an alternative. Aim to get the target audience to share the link for the experience with other at-risk youth.

Success would be finding a headline or tagline and a hashtag that these youths could get behind. The challenge is that your campaign message must have the same power to attract this group's attention and must be delivered in the channels they pay attention to. ■

Fabiola Veronica is a Sao Paulo–based creative director who specializes in all aspects of design. Her experience allows her to develop creative solutions for print, digital, and interactive marketing campaigns. In addition to her technical skills, Fabiola applies conceptual thinking and digital strategy, allowing her to present a broader platform of solutions for clients.

ASSIGNMENT: Create a launch campaign for an established brand of your choice looking to enter the South American market with a new service. Think Ralph Lauren, Bloomingdale's, or Rent the Runway goes to Brazil. The service is a virtual personal stylist and it is still very foreign to many in the region, so as a result it has an air of exclusivity. Most think that it could only be affordable to the "rich and famous." How would you use or change this label? Either way, it is your job to create a digital strategy to make this a success. You'll be judged on how you would create a market for this service through awareness and presenting the features and benefits. What channels and phases can you design to make this service sustainable? What social media tools or platforms would you use to engage in conversation with potential new users in this new market? How

would you use events, promotional items, and partnerships to increase the exposure of this brand? Lastly, how would you measure each channel and tactic to gauge the efficacy of the campaign? The metrics you'll need to measure are number of followers, amount of traffic, and new subscribers to the new service. ■

Hajime Yoshida is a freelance graphic designer working in the Tokyo fashion and music industries. In April 2015, he started Sasanqua Design Incorporated, a firm focused on the social role of graphic design. Sasanqua specializes in consulting, brand strategy, marketing, and design for educational and medical institutions such as colleges, high schools, hospitals, and medical trading companies.

ASSIGNMENT: Choose a university or college and rebrand it. Create a new logo, copy, and ads for awareness targeting the places its potential students would see them. In many countries, a declining birthrate has been a social problem. Universities and colleges have suffered from a decline in enrollment numbers and have been facing the dilemma of going commercial to get more students or keeping their enrollment selective. You should solve the problem with a tone that balances between appealing to more students and communicating the high academic standards required upon admission. Remember you have to follow the educational philosophy from the university's heritage while reimagining its design. ■

Michael J. Miraflor has worked at a media agency for his entire career, but thinks of himself as more a student of culture and technology. Born in Los Angeles, his upbringing in a first-generation Filipino-American family had him seeking identity through Little League Baseball and hip hop. After graduating from UC–Berkeley in 2004, he's had the pleasure and good luck of working at Freestyle Interactive (SF), Deep Focus (BK/NYC), and ZenithOptimedia (NYC). He's currently Head of Strategy for Blue 449 in the Americas, and a Global Executive MBA candidate at the Berlin School of Creative Leadership.

ASSIGNMENT: List three mobile applications that you use on a daily basis. Take note of when these applications update to new versions, and write down what has changed. This can include a range from small (e.g., tweaks to the mechanics, extra tools) to large (e.g., change of the app logo, major additions or subtractions from user interface). Take note of the changes that you have noticed on your own. Then read the description of the update from the app developer, and note any announced changes that you did not notice yourself. On a spreadsheet, list out all of these changes in a single column. On an adjacent column, line up what you think the reason is for the app developer to change the feature. Repeat this through at least one (and up to three) months, tracking whether the app developer is continuing to address already tracked features, or introducing new changes.

By the end of your study you should have three very different spreadsheets for the three different apps you have tracked. Ask yourself: Why do they look so different? Why would one app tweak a single feature repeatedly, while others had less focus and address a laundry list of items? For each update, decide on whether it was proactive (e.g., product iteration to improve the user experience) or reactive (e.g., a necessary change because users weren't happy). Evaluate what you think the fortunes of each app are (in the greater context of the app owner's operation) taking into consideration the proactive or reactive nature of their updates. Is this a leading or trailing indicator of growth or decline? At the end of this exercise, perhaps without knowing it, you have extrapolated the product strategy behind each application. Take this information and create a campaign to increase downloads of one of these three apps. Use the information you learned about the target and their behavior to select at least three channels to execute. ∎

Born and raised on the small island of St. Vincent, **Shayne Alexander** moved to NYC to pursue his advertising dreams. He got his start in photography and brings this eye to his art direction duties at BBDO NY. In addition to advertising, Shayne is also an awarded DJ. He won Heineken's Green Synergy Competition in St. Vincent in 2009. Since then, Shayne received recognition from the Advertising Club of New York and won The One Club's Creative Boot Camp in 2014.

ASSIGNMENT: You've just been asked to take on a new brief.

Product: For the money, the 2017 Dodge Dart is one of the best options you could find in the market of a small sedan that offers roominess, ample feature content, and abundant style.

Problem: 21–30-year-old males don't find the Dodge Dart "cool" enough for them. They think its a dad's car. Get: 21–30-year-old males to love the Dodge Dart as the coolest car they could have. Idea starters: Cool car, gets the girl. Right; but go farther than that to define the approach with attitude. As time passes, adjust the make and model of the car. ■

ASSIGNMENT: Your client is a brand manufacturer who has been selling to their end consumers through distribution channels for several years. Due to an increasingly competitive market landscape they've now decided to begin selling their products directly to their consumers through an online retail website and with an aggressive advertising campaign (in digital and traditional channels). Create a solution that drives qualified consumer traffic to their new e-commerce site without alienating their existing sales distribution partners. *As an example, think of an electronics brand that primarily sells through large retailers such as Target, Walmart, Costco, etc.* ■

During the past 12 years **Andy Long** has led business development and strategy for a variety of companies ranging from startups to Inc. 500 brands to Fortune 500 companies. As a partner at Denver, Colorado–based Interstellar (*www.gointerstellar.com*). Andy brings his experience as a top-performing sales leader and brand strategist to his role as senior vice president of business development and strategic partnerships for Interstellar. With a focus on building integrated partnerships with brands and software platforms alike, Andy is a textbook Malcolm Gladwell "connector." His unique ability to quickly develop meaningful relationships and solve problems has helped Interstellar solidify their position as a top digital partner in the Denver Metro region and beyond.

Formerly of Brooklyn, **Louisa McCabe** is now living in Brittany, France, working for editorial and marketing clients and writing a book on typography. With her love of great writing and exceptional photography, her approach to design tells the story of the publication, organization, or business in creative and relatable ways.

ASSIGNMENT: For a designer interested in editorial work, I recommend the following project: Choose an existing title—for instance, *Vogue*, *ESPN*, *Fast Company*, *Complex*—and it helps if it is in your area of interest. Your task is to design a small supplement to the magazine. This supplement will be targeted at a particular demographic within the title's larger demographic. For instance, a supplement to *ESPN* could be about the Olympics, one for *Vogue* could focus on up-and-coming designers in China, one for *Complex* could focus on Kendrick Lamar's new album and his place in hip hop history. The supplement will tell an expanded story to your particular readers. You are demonstrating in your portfolio that you are *au fait* with the magazine's content, its readers, and its advertisers. Supplements are rarely created without an advertising sponsor, and designers who understand economic relationships are valued. When you design the supplement (say, eight pages) you are not slavishly following the magazine's style, but creating a "cousin style." It is recognizably from the magazine's stable but also has its own look, photographic style, and typography. This is a chance to highlight your typographic skills. Use type in a clear, creative, and unusual way. Include a cover, table of contents, intro page, and couple of stories—basically a variety of pages. You do not need real copy but you should include real headlines. For the print version, make the page size smaller than the full magazine. Create stylish and unconfusing pages. Design the supplement for print, tablet, and smartphone—redesigning the content for each format both horizontally and vertically—which will demonstrate your ability to repurpose content in a variety of formats. Create PDFs to mock-up the pages for smartphone and tablet. Finally, create some digital banners to flag the upcoming supplement on Facebook and on the magazine website. Target your readers and use the type and photography that you have already developed. ■

David Quintiliani is a creative director whose understanding of emerging technologies has helped him reimagine how traditional brands find their voice (without losing their soul) in the new digital world. He believes that social media, the post-TV landscape, and the trend toward brands as publishers has opened the door to a new advertising that not only benefits from authenticity, but depends on it.

ASSIGNMENT: Redefine a familiar brand as a publisher or distributor of content. Red Bull, for example, used to sell energy drinks. Now they are a record label that breaks new talent, a video network of extreme sports, and a publisher of serious music journalism. Assignment: Select a known brand, consider their core audience, and create a credible plan for creating, licensing, and distributing content in a way that will build deeper loyalty and encourage brand advocacy without pushing product. ■

Gail Anderson is a New York–based designer, writer, educator, and partner at Anderson Newton Design. From 2002 through 2010, Gail served as Creative Director of Design at SpotCo, a New York City advertising agency that creates artwork for Broadway and institutional theater. From 1987 to early 2002, she worked at *Rolling Stone* magazine, serving as associate art director, deputy art director, and finally as the magazine's senior art director. Anderson is the author of *Outside the Box*, for Princeton Architectural Press, as well as co-author of ten books with Steven Heller. She has contributed to design books, publications, and blogs worldwide. Anderson teaches at the School of Visual Arts, and serves on The Citizens' Stamp Advisory Committee for the United States Postal Service and on the board for the Type Directors Club. She is the recipient of the 2008 Lifetime Achievement Medal from the AIGA, and her work is in the permanent collection of the Cooper Hewitt, the Library of Congress, and the Milton Glaser Design Archives at SVA.

ASSIGNMENT: Branding a Neighborhood

Spend an afternoon walking through interesting neighborhoods in your city or town. Find the small pockets of communities that are up-and-coming— or are established, but little-known. What can you do to build enthusiasm about an area, to attract locals to participate in events or patronize local establishments? How do you create a buzz and make a place "cool" for its inhabitants? This assignment is about branding a neighborhood, so choosing will be part of the fun. Don't go for someplace obvious like Williamsburg— that's already well-established and has a high "coolness" factor that at this point verges on overkill. Is there an area that has great theaters? A spot that feels particularly kid-friendly? A snippet of town that has really interesting architecture? You will be asked to create a name for your location if there isn't already one (also part of the fun), so bear that in mind as you walk around. Your deliverables will include a logo for your neighborhood, as well as a landing page and four additional screens for a community website or blog about the area. You'll also create promotional materials for an event that celebrates your special place, like a pub crawl, concert series, or street fair. Are you making posters that hang in local restaurants? An app that takes you on a walking tour of your neighborhood? Think big and have fun. The ultimate goal is to get local residents to celebrate their environment—though attracting visitors to the area is never a bad thing. But don't think about it as tourism—keep it small-scale and focused on the heart of your community. But I repeat, THINK BIG (in terms of what you create to attract eyeballs and bodies) and have fun! ■

Contact Me!

Lastly, I don't know the right answer but I know what I think. I'm not a writer but I have something to say. The opinions, methods, and stories in this book are *my* right answers to this point and I appreciate being able to share them with you. I would love to hear your stories, adventures, wins, and losses applying any of the material; e-mail *me@douglasdavis.com* and visit *www.thinkhowtheythink.com*. Thank you so much.

ABOUT THE AUTHOR

Douglas Davis, Principal: The Davis Group LLC & Associate Professor
@douglasQdavis
douglasdavis.com
thinkhowtheythink.com

Brooklyn-based Douglas Davis enjoys being one of the variety of voices needed in front of and behind the concept, marketing plan, or digital strategy. His approach to creativity combines right-brained creative problem-solving with left-brained strategic thinking. The unique mix of creative strategy, integrated marketing, and art direction is what Douglas brings into the classroom. Douglas began his teaching career as an adjunct in tandem with his professional career, following in the footsteps of his mentors at Pratt Institute who worked during the day and taught at night. Currently, he is an associate professor within the Communication Design department at New York City College of Technology in Brooklyn.

Douglas is a former adjunct professor at New York University in the Master's in Integrated Marketing program and current adjunct associate professor at City College in the Branding and Integrated Communications (BIC) program. As a HOW Design university contributor, his ideas have been presented in webinar, conference, and course format. His online class, Creative Strategy and the Business of Design, has been well received by a mix of creative professionals practicing in the United States and beyond. Digital Marketer, Freelance Art and Creative Director, Advertising & Design Educator . . . who depends on what day.

In 2011 Douglas founded The Davis Group LLC and continues to offer strategic solutions to client branding, digital, and design problems. In addition to client work and giving back in the classroom, Douglas was appointed to serve on the advisory board for New York City's High School for Innovation in Advertising and Media (iAM). His advertising and academic experience aided him in authoring the four-year curriculum for the first public advertising high school in the country. Following the launch of iAM, Douglas contributed as an education consultant for the launch of the Manhattan Early College School for Advertising (MECA).

Douglas holds a BA in Graphic Design from Hampton University, an MS in Communications Design from Pratt Institute, and an MS in Integrated Marketing from New York University.

INDEX

Note: Entries in **bold** indicate business terms to know.